2001

✓Read

Interest rates low,
    STocks prices will grow
Interest rates high,
    Stock prices will die

Advance praise for the first edition of
INVESTING IN IPOs

"The Internet and other technologies are providing a sea of new opportunities for individual investors. . . . **THIS INFORMATIVE BOOK MAKES IT POSSIBLE FOR INVESTORS TO SIZE UP THE QUALITY AND GROWTH POTENTIAL OF THE IPOS THEY ARE INTERESTED IN.** I recommend reading *Investing in IPOs* by Tom Taulli before you start buying."

ANDREW D. KLEIN
Founder & Chief Strategist, Wit Capital Corporation

"Tom Taulli has done an exceptional job of demystifying IPOs for investors with all levels of expertise. **THIS BOOK IS LONG OVERDUE!**"

JOHN E. FITZGIBBON, JR.
Editor, *IPO Reporter*

"Tom Taulli has written the essential guide for investors who are puzzled by what IPOs are and how they work. The best investment strategies, the potential risks, and knowing when to get out once an IPO has fizzled—it's all here. . . . **YOU'D BE FOOLISH TO ENTER THE IPO MARKET WITHOUT READING THIS BOOK FIRST.**"

DAVID B. BATSTONE
Editor-at-Large, *Business 2.0*

"Tom Taulli has written **A COMPREHENSIVE AND INVALUABLE BOOK** on investing in initial public offerings for the individual investor. Not only does Taulli explain the IPO process from the beginning to end, but he also includes valuable information on how to access free research on the Internet, read a prospectus, and understand IPO risk factors."

LINDA R. KILLIAN
Principal, Renaissance Capital Corporation

Investing in
IPOs
Version 2.0

Also available from

BLOOMBERG PRESS

Investing in Small-Cap Stocks:
Revised Edition
by Christopher Graja and Elizabeth Ungar, Ph.D.

Zero Gravity Version 2.0
Launching Technology Companies
in a Tougher Venture Capital World
by Steve Harmon
(June 2001)

Investing in Hedge Funds:
Strategies for the New Marketplace
by Joseph G. Nicholas

Small-Cap Dynamics
by Satya Dev Pradhuman

Stock Options: Getting Your Share of the Action
Negotiating Shares and Terms in Incentive
and Nonqualified Plans
by Tom Taulli

A complete list of our titles is available at
WWW.BLOOMBERG.COM/BOOKS

ATTENTION CORPORATIONS

BLOOMBERG PRESS BOOKS are available at quantity discounts with bulk purchase for sales promotional use and for corporate education or other business uses. Special editions or book excerpts can also be created. For information, please call 609-279-4670 or write to: Special Sales Dept., Bloomberg Press, P.O. Box 888, Princeton, NJ 08542.

BLOOMBERG PERSONAL BOOKSHELF

Investing in
IPOs
Version 2.0
REVISED AND UPDATED EDITION

TOM TAULLI

FOREWORD BY STEVE HARMON

BLOOMBERG PRESS

PRINCETON

This publication contains the author's opinions and is designed to provide accurate and authoritative information. It is sold with the understanding that the author, publisher, and Bloomberg L.P. are not engaged in rendering legal, accounting, investment-planning, or other professional advice. The reader should seek the services of a qualified professional for such advice; the author, publisher, and Bloomberg L.P. cannot be held responsible for any loss incurred as a result of specific investments or planning decisions made by the reader.

First edition published 2001
1 3 5 7 9 10 8 6 4 2

Library of Congress Cataloging-in-Publication Data

Taulli, Tom, 1968–
    Investing in IPOs / Tom Taulli ; foreword by Steve Harmon. –Version 2.0
        p. cm. - -   (Bloomberg personal bookshelf)
    Includes index.
    ISBN 1-57660-046-7 (alk. paper)
        1. Going public (Securities) 2. Investments. I. Title: IPOs. II. Title.
    III. Series

    HG4028.S7 T38 2001
    332.63'22 - - dc21

                                                    00-048574

Edited by Tracy Tait
Book design by Don Morris Design

To my parents,
Tom and Anne Taulli,
who allowed me to
pursue my crazy ideas

FOREWORD
by Steve Harmon **xiii**

INTRODUCTION 1

PART I

Introducing IPOs **10**

CHAPTER 1
IPO Basics
Introducing initial public offerings **12**

CHAPTER 2
The IPO Process
*A step-by-step tour—from number crunching
to the effective date* **30**

PART II

IPOs for Investors **44**

CHAPTER 3
Finding the Best IPO Information
*The most reliable IPO intelligence, including
Web sites, newsletters, and magazines* **46**

CHAPTER 4
Making Sense of the Prospectus
*Decoding the fine print: how to size up past
performance and future prospects* **66**

CHAPTER 5
Risk Factors
A checklist of warning signs and red flags **84**

CHAPTER 6
IPO Investment Strategies
*Simple, commonsense guidelines and
more sophisticated techniques* **98**

PART III
Important IPO Sectors **112**

CHAPTER 7
Technology IPOs
*Prospecting for high-tech winners: Internet,
software, and telecom stocks* **114**

CHAPTER 8
Biotech IPOs
*Decoding a major market force of the future
and understanding its risks* **130**

CHAPTER 9
Finance Sector IPOs
*Banking, brokerage, mutual fund, and
insurance industry offerings* **144**

CHAPTER 10
Retail Sector IPOs
Spotting the lasting trends in the market **158**

CHAPTER 11
Foreign IPOs
Profiting from growth on a global scale **166**

PART IV

Other IPO Investments 178

CHAPTER 12
IPO Mutual Funds
*Spotting the funds that invest the most and best
in initial public offerings* **180**

CHAPTER 13
Virtual IPOs
*Online pioneering efforts from
investment community entrepreneurs* **192**

CHAPTER 14
Spin-offs
How and why companies spin off, and how to invest **210**

CHAPTER 15
Fad IPOs
*Assessing short-term profit opportunities while
avoiding the inevitable price plunge* **220**

CHAPTER 16
Stock Options and IPOs
Mastering the new standard in employee compensation **230**

CONCLUSION **241**

APPENDIX A:
The Underwriting Process **248**

APPENDIX B:
Analyzing the Financial Statement Items **250**

RESOURCES **254**

NOTES **261**

GLOSSARY **262**

INDEX **273**

Initial Public Offering (IPO): The first time in a company's history that public investors are able to purchase stock in the company. This is a huge accomplishment for a company, and in many cases there is a greater demand for shares than can be satisfied by the number of shares being offered. Investors who buy shares of an IPO seek the opportunities and assume the risks of participating at this early stage of a company's growth.

ACKNOWLEDGMENTS

THIS BOOK WOULD not have been possible without the help of many people. I'm grateful for the tremendous help from Larrie Weil, the chief of Corporate Finance at Southwest Securities; Andrew D. Klein, the founder of the innovative online investment bank Wit Capital Corporation; Nadine Wong, the publisher of the biotech newsletter *BioTech Navigator;* Linda Killian, the portfolio manager of the IPO Fund; Peter Schwartz, the founder of FreeEDGAR.com; Deborah Monrue, Tom Madden, and Jeff Stacey from IPO Monitor.com; Drew Field, the leader in the direct IPO field; Jay Sears, the vice president of marketing and business development at EDGAR Online; Tom Stewart-Gordon, the editor of the *SCOR Report;* Internet guru Steve Harmon; Bill Hambrecht, the founder of WR Hambrecht + Co; Walter Cruttenden, the cofounder of E*Offering; and Frank Marino, the CEO of NetCap Ventures.

Finally, I would like to thank my business partner, Matt Harris, who had much patience while I wrote this book.

FOREWORD

NVESTOR ARDOR FOR initial public offerings waxes and wanes with the fortunes of technology stocks. When tech stocks are hot, everyone wants one at IPO. When tech is out of favor, investors who were once lining up for IPOs—like moviegoers at a box-office blockbuster standing in line to spend $20 on a ticket, soda, and popcorn—start to wonder what they were thinking (and why they are paying more for the snacks than for the film).

Despite efforts and promises made by a host of Internet brokerages and start-ups to "level the playing field," the fact remains that IPOs are still mostly the exclusive domain of institutional investors. The Internet has the power to change that, but it has yet to do so to any great degree. Allocations of IPOs from brokerages to individual investors are a substantial minority of the overall offering, an afterthought from the underwriters, who have to carve out big positions for the large accounts that generate order flow. Is it totally hopeless? What can you do to increase your chances of landing an IPO?

We've seen attempts such as Bill Hambrecht's OpenIPO try to bring an auction model to the IPO process, to bring the individual investor to the table. The simple goal: allow individual investors to bid on new offerings. Hambrecht's effort has been notable but has not replaced the traditional IPO as we know it. First, an auction model may price out the usual first-day pop that initially attracts investors. In other words, auctions can be too efficient sometimes—pegging the price and leaving nothing on the upside out of the gate. Second, companies going public rely on the underwriter's established distribution chains—the brokers who can sell the deal—to provide a level of assurance that the cash they so desperately need from the IPO can be raised quickly.

Other attempts, mostly by relative unknowns, have been made to offer IPOs directly through the Web. One drawback is that most of those offerings tend to be highly speculative. And hovering over such speculations is the inevitable question: couldn't they get a better underwriter—a traditional underwriter?

Throughout 1999 and into spring 2000 the Internet fever that spread globally also focused a lot of attention on venture capital—where higher risk can lead to higher returns. Long-standing stocks, such as CMGI (which I called at 50¢ a share in 1996), became prominent in 1999 as ordinary investors flocked into stocks with venture capital exposure. Average investors were tired of hearing about how venture firms posted 1,000 to 10,000 percent returns on a ridiculous dot-dumb idea. In 1999, too many of those investors became enamored with venture capital.

This led to the rise of companies such as Garage.com, Offroad Capital, and others who promise to put at least accredited investors into private investments. It's too soon to gauge their success, but average investors have lost their voracious appetite for venture deals—for now and for the near term.

The important thing to understand here is that individual investors often take venture risk in IPOs, since many companies going public are neither earnings rich nor earnings positive. Part of the tech meltdown in April 2000 occurred because too many venture-stage companies were being taken public. It became a parade of offerings that wouldn't have survived the 1970s TV classic *The Gong Show*. And by August 2000, plenty of investors had been gonged themselves—by venture risk and the floodgate IPO parade of 1999. This created a more discerning investor, and a scarred one at that.

BACK UP A FEW STEPS and it's clear that the trend toward retail investing is the single biggest event now altering the investment landscape. In early 2000 *USA Today* reported that 34 percent of equity investors in the United States owned Internet stocks. More and more pension funds own technology stocks. And as technology continues to permeate society, workers are demanding increased exposure to the emerging growth they see around them.

It is no accident that the rise of the Nasdaq since 1989 has been driven by technology. The obvious seeds had been planted in the 1970s by PC pioneers such as Bill Gates, Paul Allen, Gary Kildall, and dozens of others. It is interesting to note, though, that another tech seed had been planted even earlier, in the late 1960s. That one—the Internet—would also have an enormous impact, ironically after PCs.

The Internet as we now know it is a far cry from the kluge it was back then. In 1969 Vint Cerf and a few friends at UCLA tinkered with creating the foundation for a computer network under the sanction of the U.S. government, which was trying to create a global network for communications that could survive nuclear holocaust. Their tinkering led to the development of the Internet.

Thirty years later the more consumer-friendly Internet and PC met and realized they were each part of a larger financial picture. The elements were all in place—a global communication network, widespread technology adoption (35 percent of U.S. households owned a PC and one-third of investors owned technology stocks directly), the proliferation of online brokerages (led by E*TRADE and Schwab), the accessibility of stock research on the Web, and a level of security that allows for secure online transactions. The Internet enabled a plethora of new companies to be started and go public. Any willing average investor was one click away from retirement if he bought the right IPOs.

Not all IPOs are created equal, however. And many investors today are thankfully more careful about the stocks they want to own—that's a message I want to emphasize. Yes, the market still rewards some investors who chase the latest trend or fad. But be careful. Knowing the process of the IPO is what Tom Taulli's book is all about. It's also about the places and uses of the Internet, so you can be more knowledgeable as you navigate in that environment. Taking the IPO investing route is fraught with peril, and knowledge is your best protection from the daily hype that can easily sweep investors into a lemming mentality. In the information economy, knowledge is king, and this book will give you an excellent introduction into the IPO process. Use it to your advantage. Ignore it at your risk.

> — STEVE HARMON
> Author of *Zero Gravity: Riding Venture Capital from High-Tech Start-up to Breakout IPO*

INTRODUCTION

ITH THE
Web expanding exponentially, the telecom infrastructure has been under incredible stress. Can the
current infrastructure support the rapid expansion
rate of the Web, while itself attempting to grow at an
equal pace? In the past few years a variety of companies
have emerged to develop cutting-edge equipment that
will help enhance the speed and capacity of the telecom infrastructure, thus addressing this issue.

One such company is Sycamore Networks Inc.
(SCMR), founded in February 1998. The mastermind
behind this software-based optical networking products
company is a legend of high tech: Gururaj Deshpande.
In 1991 he founded Cascade Communications Corp.,
a computer networking company. By 1997 the company had $500 million in revenues and 900 employees,
and in 1997 he sold the company to Ascend Communications for $3.7 billion. Besides having great business

savvy, he also has great technology credentials, including a Ph.D. in data communications.

Deshpande understood that if Sycamore Networks was to succeed against the giants—Cisco, Nortel, and Lucent—he needed a tremendous management team. So he hired Dan Smith, who was the president and CEO of Cascade Communications Corp., as the CEO of Sycamore Networks. It was under Smith's leadership that Cascade Communications experienced its hypergrowth, and he would lead Sycamore through the same.

In October 1999, Sycamore Networks went public at $38 per share. On its first day of trading, the shares soared to $184.75. In a few weeks, the shares were at $300, and the market value of the company was in excess of $30 billion.

Since then, the stock has split twice. A $10,000 investment in the IPO would now be worth $102,000.

Of course, Sycamore Networks was not the only hot IPO. In fact, it has become common to see big surges in the IPO market. Here are some of the top IPOs for 2000 (as of the end of July):

Company	Growth
◆ Sonus Networks, Inc. (SONS)	730.98 percent
◆ New Focus Inc. (NUFO)	583.13 percent
◆ Nuance Communications (NUAN)	573.53 percent
◆ Turnstone Systems, Inc. (TSTN)	510.78 percent
◆ Orchid Biosciences, Inc. (ORCH)	498.44 percent
◆ webMethods, Inc. (WEBM)	405.71 percent
◆ Quantum Effect Devices, Inc. (QEDI)	400.78 percent
◆ StorageNetworks, Inc. (STOR)	369.21 percent
◆ Marvell Technology Group Ltd. (MRVL)	355.83 percent
◆ Bookham Technology (BKHM)	348.52 percent

But in 2000 there was also a dark side to IPOs. When the Nasdaq plunged in April 2000, so did many IPOs. Some were even crushed. In turn, investors wanted to focus on companies that promised more safety, companies with solid business models. There was very little willingness to take bets on concept companies.

Here's a look at some of the worst:

Company	Growth
◆ drkoop.com (KOOP)	-95.92 percent
◆ VarsityBooks.com Inc. (VSTY)	-86.88 percent
◆ ImproveNet, Inc. (IMPV)	-86.72 percent
◆ Pets.com, Inc. (IPET)	-83.81 percent
◆ Uproar Inc. (UPRO)	-83.21 percent
◆ Healthgate Data Corp. (HGAT)	-82.39 percent
◆ Firstworld Communications, Inc. (FWIS)	-78.68 percent
◆ Shochet Holding Corp. (SHOC)	-77.78 percent
◆ ActivCard SA (ACTI)	-77.12 percent
◆ FASTNET Corporation (FSST)	-76.04 percent

However, don't let the numbers scare you away—by summer 2000, the IPO market began to roar back. And the lesson learned is that it is now more critical than ever that before investing in IPOs, you need to do your homework. It's a fact that IPOs make one of the best places in the financial markets to find huge gainers. There's enormous upside if you can manage to pick the winners at the right time. Yes, it's a tricky and risky feat—but this book was written to bring investors closer to solving the puzzle.

You may have heard that IPOs are allocated first to wealthy individuals and institutions. It's true; those with a large capital base typically have first pick of IPOs. This is the case with any type of investment, even though the situation is changing as the Internet brings us all closer to investment opportunities. But the playing field is not equal yet—being wealthy still carries its privileges.

For example, in 1995 Michael Jordan, the star basketball player for the Chicago Bulls, was able to purchase 217,392 shares of the Oakley IPO, because he endorsed the company's sunglasses. Then there was Demi Moore, who was the recipient of about 650,000 shares of the Planet Hollywood IPO at the offering price. (This turned out to be not as good as it sounded. The company eventually went bust.)

However, with the emergence of the Internet, individual investors are starting to participate more and more in IPOs. For example, Wit Capital allowed investors to participate in the IPOs of Internet Capital Group (ICGE) and Nuance Communications (NUAN). WR Hambrecht made it possible for its subscribers to buy shares in Sonus Networks (SONS) and DigitalThink (DTHK). Some opportunities are there for the taking.

Also, you don't need to invest on the first day to make money in IPOs. For example, the institutions and wealthy individuals that purchase IPOs usually do so to generate a quick profit. This is known as flipping. While a one-day 50 percent or more profit is tremendous, you may be missing out on much more upside still to come. Consider those investors who flipped the Microsoft offering. Of course, they have regretted it ever since.

Successful IPO investing involves being patient. The only way to get rich overnight is through the lottery or inheritance. Besides, short-term investing is a game for professionals, who have the time and resources to devote their life to investing. Playing against them is very dangerous to the survival of your portfolio.

However, being an individual investor also has many advantages in the IPO world. Since the IPO market consists mostly of small companies, much of Wall Street will probably ignore these newer companies. Wall Street likes covering the big players, such as Microsoft, Exxon, and IBM. Normally an IPO has but a few analysts covering it (and in some cases, none). This gives the individual investor an edge, since the IPO stock may not fully reflect what's happening to the company.

Another advantage to investing in IPOs is that analysis is much easier. It does not take as much work to study a small company, which may have only a few products or services, as it does to understand a multinational company that has its hands in a variety of industries. These factors do not mean that investing in IPOs is simple or that there is a "secret formula" for finding big gains. Rather, it requires a large amount of work. But remember—it is worth it.

Of course, IPOs can be extremely risky. There are many IPOs that have collapsed—the value of some of them has been reduced to pennies. After all, small companies can be adversely affected by numerous factors, including a top manager who bails out or a major customer that goes to another vendor. But this book will help you screen IPOs and decide which opportunities to take and which to quickly and firmly pass by. Investing in IPOs can be a wild ride.

IPOs are unpredictable, but then again, buying the "nobrainer" blue-chip stocks can be risky, too. Just look at the performances of International Harvester, United Fruit,

Pennsylvania Railroad, Woolworth's, and Western Union. Let's consider another example: you could have bought U.S. Steel in 1959 for $100 per share. At that time, it was a bellwether. Everyone marveled at it as a symbol of America's strength. It was a company that, when there was a labor strike, would get the attention of the President of the United States. Despite its past prestige, by 1993 the stock was selling for less than $50 per share. Even seemingly super-growth stocks can have stunning losses, such as Oracle's 30 percent one-day drop in late 1997.

As with any effective investment strategy, the way to deal with risk is to diversify. You might, for example (depending on your risk profile), invest 5 percent of your net worth in IPOs. You can then allocate the rest of your funds in other asset classes, such as blue chips, bonds, or gold.

In fact, chances are that you have already participated in the IPO market and don't realize it. How is this possible? The reason is that mutual funds are the biggest purchasers of IPOs. For example, Fidelity constitutes 10 percent of the IPO market share in the United States. So if you own mutual funds, you likely own IPOs.

Also, you might be an employee of a company that in the future will go public. A major trend in compensation is the granting of stock options—a tremendous motivator for employees. If a company does go public, the owners of these stock options stand to make a great deal of money. So it's important to understand the IPO game. You don't want to lose what could potentially become millions of dollars.

Despite what you might hear, you do not need a degree from the Wharton School of Business to successfully invest in IPOs (in fact, it might help if you don't have such a degree). Top-name investors such as Warren Buffett, Peter Lynch, and Michael Price all tout simple strategies. Leave the complicated intricacies of hedging to the pros.

This book will provide you with easy-to-understand strategies for taking advantage of the opportunities in the IPO market. The analysis involves both quantitative and qualitative factors. We will dig into financial statements. We will study risk factors. We will look at market growth of important IPO sectors such as high-tech and financial services. We will investigate the backgrounds of manage-ment. We will see how solid the underwriter is. We'll even present the best sources of IPO intelligence and market research.

And as you gain a better understanding of the IPO mar-ket, you will see that it is very exciting. You have the oppor-tunity to investigate cutting-edge companies that are reshaping the economy. You will be glimpsing the prod-ucts and services of the future.

Within a very short period, the investment world has undergone revolutionary change that gives you and me access to investments that were once only available to big financial institutions. What you make of these opportuni-ties is entirely up to you. It's now just a matter of doing your homework before you invest.

Let's get started.

G. Sachs – underwriter

Credit Suisse

INTRODUCING
IPOs

PART

I

CHAPTER

IPO
BASICS

I T'S A COMMON MISCONCEPTION that IPOs are a guaranteed road to riches. Although there are many IPOs that do extremely well, the fact is that IPOs are like any other investment: there are no guarantees. Before considering IPO investment strategies, it's important for investors to understand what IPOs are and how they work.

Anyone reading this book probably knows that an initial public offering (IPO) is the first sale of stock by a company to the public. It's when a company makes the transformation from being privately held to becoming publicly traded, complete with its own ticker symbol. However, there's probably a lot of other, more advanced IPO terminology that most people don't know. For example: What does it mean when an IPO goes "effective"? What is the registration statement? What is the "red herring"? What exactly do the underwriters do? These questions—plus a great deal more about investing in IPOs—are covered in this book.

This chapter takes a look at what motivates a company to launch an initial public offering. We will also meet the major players in the IPO process.

WHY DO COMPANIES GO PUBLIC?

THERE IS NO single answer to that question. It's a major decision that will surely change the character of a company and mean many sleepless nights for management. What's more, an IPO is very expensive. ✓ The company will need to hire attorneys, accountants, printers, and many other advisers described later in this chapter.

These are the main reasons a company might decide to go public:

PRESTIGE

AN IPO IS A *major* accomplishment. Wall Street will suddenly begin to take notice. Analysts will start following the
company; so will the press. And hiring new employees will
become easier, because publicly traded companies are
generally perceived to be more stable than private companies. In fact, the company might even choose to offer
employee stock options as compensation or as part of a
retirement plan. Management benefits from offering stock
option incentives through tax advantages and by conserv-
ing cash flow. In addition, stock incentives can cement an
employee's stake in the company.

GETTING RICH

STAGING AN IPO is one of the best ways for company principals to get rich. For example, in April 1994 Christopher
Klaus founded Internet Services Systems (ISS) from his
grandmother's guest room. He started the company while
he was a student at Georgia Institute of Technology. He
developed shareware—called Internet Scanner—that
allows companies to protect their computer networks. His
first client, an Italian company, paid him $1,000. Then,
through a referral from his lawyer, Klaus contacted Kevin
O'Connor, the founder of another hot Internet company,
DoubleClick. O'Connor invested $50,000 in Klaus's com-
pany, a stake that is now worth $26 million.

From there ISS grew at an astronomical rate, moving
from $257,000 in sales in 1995 to $13 million in 1997, and
the number of employees surged from 7 to 141. When his
company went public in early 1998, Klaus owned 26.1 percent of the stock. Within a week, this twenty-four-year-old
was worth a mind-boggling $160 million. Yes, enough
money to pay off his school loans.

However, it's not just the founders who get rich; a
company's employees can, too. Microsoft has created
more than 2,000 millionaires because of stock options.
Another example is Apple Computer, which went public
in 1980: on the first day of trading, forty employees

became instant millionaires. ✓

And, of course, need I remind the reader that anyone could have bought shares in Microsoft, ISS, and Apple on the open market? If you had bought 1,000 shares of Microsoft in <u>1986, by November 30, 1998</u>, you would have <u>been worth $8,784,000.</u>

CASH INFUSION

AN IPO WILL TYPICALLY raise a lot of cash for a company. This money does not have to be paid back. It can be used to build new facilities, fund research and development, and float the acquisition of a new or expanded business.

Some examples:

No more

◆ **United Parcel Service (UPS).** This is the country's largest delivery company. After being private for nearly 100 years, the company decided to go public in November 1999. In its offering, the company raised a staggering $5.4 billion.

◆ **Arrowpoint Communications (ARPT).** This company was only a few years old when it went public in late March 2000. In 1999, the company had sales of $12.3 million. In the IPO, Arrowpoint raised an impressive $170 million. Then in early May 2000, networking equipment maker Cisco Systems Inc. (CSCO) bought Arrowpoint. The price tag? About $5.7 billion.

All this was cash raised from initial public offerings.

LIQUIDITY

OVERALL, BECAUSE OF the large amount of capital raised from an offering, an IPO gives a company the increased ability to raise even more money. For example, banks are more willing to lend money and extend credit to publicly traded companies. And stock can be used as collateral for loans, a practice used by Lawrence Ellison, the founder of Oracle, for many of the company's early years.

An IPO also allows the founders to diversify their holdings. For example, in the ISS IPO, Klaus sold 100,000 shares of his stock and Kevin O'Connor sold 55,000 shares. This transaction was legitimate, but be wary of founders selling a large amount of stock at the time of the IPO. This is what is known as a 'bailout' and may be an indication of a bad offering. After all, the founders know whether the company has sound prospects for growth.

In some instances the founders don't sell any of their own shares, as was the case with Yahoo! The cofounders, Jerry Yang and David Filo, did not unload any of their 4,003,750 shares.

STOCK AS CURRENCY

ANOTHER MAJOR ADVANTAGE of an IPO is that a company can use its stock as currency to purchase other businesses. Because of the lack of liquidity, and because they are hard to value, private companies often have difficulty acquiring other businesses. Suppose, for example, that a private firm wants to buy your company, but that you also have a similarly attractive offer from Microsoft. What suitor would you be more comfortable with? In most cases, your answer would be the established, recognized company.

Using stock as currency for acquisitions is a fairly common practice. For example, VeriSign Inc. (VRSN) went public in January 1998. The company is a leading provider of digital certificates, which is a technology that provides for secure online transactions. In March 2000, VeriSign Inc. purchased Network Solutions Inc. (NSOL), which registers top-level domain names worldwide. The purchase was a pure stock-for-stock deal and no cash traded hands. The price tag came to $21 billion.

HOWEVER, AN IPO is not the answer in every case. There are many reasons why a company might decide not to do an IPO. Here are some of them:

EXPENSE

DOING AN IPO is extremely expensive, but it's not just the monetary costs that are a factor. Having management divert huge amounts of time and effort preparing for the

THE COST OF AN IPO

THIS IS AN ITEMIZED LIST of costs for the IPO of RealNetworks, an Internet video/audio technology company:

Securities and Exchange Commission registration fee	$13,591
NASD filing fee	$4,985
Nasdaq national market listing fee	$50,000
Legal fees and expenses	$325,000
Accountants' fees and expenses	$225,000
Blue-sky filing and counsel fees and expenses	$5,000
Printing and engraving expenses	$150,000
Transfer agent and registrar fees	$10,000
Miscellaneous expenses	$166,424
TOTAL	$950,000

IPO can drain normal operations.

The biggest money pit that comes with an IPO is known as the underwriter's discount. This fee ranges from 5 percent to 10 percent of the amount raised in the offering. Beyond that, there are billable hours for attorneys and accountants. Printing costs (the paperwork is mind-boggling) and filing fees for both the federal government and the states in which the IPO will be offered push the bill even higher.

DOING BUSINESS AS A PUBLIC COMPANY

ONCE A COMPANY goes public, the large expenses continue. For instance, publicly traded companies are required to make certain quarterly and annual filings. They need an investor-relations department to deal with shareholder inquires and will probably need to retain attorneys and accountants to handle securities and SEC compliance matters. To handle the new reporting requirements, a company will need to implement state-of-the-art accounting and information systems.

LOSS OF PRIVACY

WHEN A COMPANY initiates an IPO, it must comply with the myriad regulations meant to protect investors. A company must disclose all "material" information. For example, in the prospectus (which is the document given to those who want to invest in an IPO), a company must disclose its financial reports, business strategies, customers, executive compensation, and risk factors. Not much is left to the imagination.

CAST OF CHARACTERS

IN ADDITION TO the company principals, many other parties take part in an IPO. Here are some of the major ones:

VENTURE CAPITALISTS

BEFORE THE IPO PROCESS can be put into motion, a company needs to attract financial support. It's several years—at least—before a start-up is ready for a public offering. The first step is for the company to seek capital from friends, family, and angels. Angels are the private investors who fund start-ups, many being entrepreneurs who have amassed fortunes by taking their own companies public and now invest in other ventures.

The boxed example on page 22 is a good illustration of several types of financing arrangements, made mostly by angels and venture capitalists.

For the most part, only high net worth individuals participate in these private transactions, because they are quite complex and risky and because they are difficult for the SEC to regulate.

For individual investors, however, it's important to note that examining early-stage financing can be useful in determining an IPO's chances for success. In the December 1996 issue of the *Journal of Finance,* Alon Brav and Paul Gompers (both well-regarded finance professors) did a comprehensive study of the performance of IPOs for companies that had venture capital and those that did not. The conclusion was that companies with VC backing over

TOP VENTURE CAPITALISTS

THE FOLLOWING ARE FOUR of the top venture capitalists and some of their investments:

- **Kleiner Perkins Caufield & Byers (www.kpcb.com).** This firm is considered the top in the field, having invested in more than 100 companies that eventually went public. The star partner at the firm is, no doubt, John Doerr. He has backed Intuit Inc. (INTU), Amazon.com Inc. (AMZN), Epicor Software Corp. (EPIC), Excite@Home Networks, Healtheon Corporation (HLTH), drugstore.com (DSCM), Homestore.com (HOMS), Martha Stewart Living Omnimedia (MSO), and Sun Microsystems Inc. (SUNW). He is also on the board of each of these companies.

- **Chase Capital Partners (www.chasecapital.com).** Since being founded in 1984, the firm has closed more than 950 transactions. Major deals include Lycos (LCOS), Puma Technology (PUMA), and StarMedia (STRM).

- **Sequoia Capital (www.sequoiacap.com).** The legendary Don Valentine, who is also founder of National Semiconductor, founded the firm in 1972. Sequoia has backed such fantastically successful companies as Cisco (CSCO), Oracle (ORCL), and Yahoo! (YHOO).

- **Benchmark Capital (www.benchmark.com).** Although a young firm (founded in 1995), Benchmark Capital has rapidly become a force. The firm has funded Red Hat (RHAT), Juniper Networks (JNPR), and CriticalPath (CPTH).

the previous five years returned, on average, 44.6 percent, compared to 22.5 percent for non–VC-backed firms.

According to the authors of that article, there are many reasons for these results. First of all, venture capital partners are typically put on the board of the company in which they are investing. The VC firm can then help provide contacts and valuable leads on additional financing. The VC firm can also attract analysts to follow the company. What's more, institutions are more comfortable buying stock from companies backed by venture capitalists.

AKAMAI: PRIVATE FINANCING HISTORY

TIM BERNERS-LEE, who invented the World Wide Web, offered a challenge to the faculty of the Massachusetts Institute of Technology (MIT) in 1995. He foresaw that the Internet would be congested unless technologies were developed to better route Internet traffic, so he challenged his colleagues to invent a new way to deliver Internet content.

Tom Leighton, a professor of applied mathematics, took the challenge. In his MIT office he mapped the Internet infrastructure and looked for the weak spots. Leighton enlisted the help of graduate student Danny Lewin and top researchers David Karger, MIT professor of electrical engineering and computer science, and Bruce Maggs, professor of computer science at Carnegie Mellon. Together, they developed advanced mathematical algorithms to speed up the Internet. Jonathan Seelig, who was enrolled in the MIT Sloan M.B.A. program, soon joined the group and helped to create a business plan.

Private financing came from the following sources:

◆ **February 1998.** This group developed a business plan and submitted it to the MIT Entrepreneurship Competition. Out of 100 entries, their business plan won the first prize of $50,000.

◆ **November 1998.** The company issued 1.1 million shares of Series A preferred stock to twenty-two investors at $7.60 per share. Top investors included Battery Ventures and Polaris Ventures.

◆ **April 1999.** The company issued 1.3 million shares of Series B preferred stock to twenty-four investors (most of these investors were from the Series A round). The stock price was $15.07.

◆ **May 1999.** The company issued senior subordinated notes (with an interest rate of 15 percent) to raise $15 million. There were also warrants to purchase 1 million shares.

◆ **October 1999.** Akamai went public at $26 per share.

STRATEGIC INVESTORS

INTERESTINGLY ENOUGH, many corporations such as AT&T, Nokia, Oracle, Cisco, Intel, Amazon.com, and even the Tribune Company are creating venture capital funds. Companies like these are known as strategic investors.

Strategic investors can be prolific, as is the case with Intel. In all, Intel Capital has funded more than 425 companies worldwide, including CMGI Inc. (CMGI), Stamps.com (STMP), and Covad Communications (COVD).

Such strategic investors are not necessarily concerned about the rate of return on their investments but usually have other considerations. In the fast-changing high-tech world, it is often difficult for large companies to innovate quickly. Investing in start-ups—companies that are known to be terrifically innovative—can be one solution for a large company. Smaller start-up companies have an advantage, since they do not have to deal with what can be a stifling bureaucracy and can focus on one product. For a big company, acquiring such a start-up can lower the risk of a new venture—assuming the start-up has already developed a product that works.

Strategic investments also can help a company extend the product line. One example is data networking product supplier Cisco Systems Inc. (CSCO), which has invested in a myriad of high-tech start-ups. In late May 1999, the company invested $13 million in a fiber-optics company, Cerent, which provides optical transport solutions. In July 1999, Cerent filed to go public. However, Cisco realized that Cerent's technology was extremely valuable for the strategic direction of Cisco and would help the company compete against Lucent, Alcatel, and Nortel Networks. So in late August 1999, Cisco bought Cerent. The price tag was huge, though, at $6.9 billion.

Oracle Ventures is another example of a strategic investor. Founded in January 1999 with $500 million, the fund was created to back companies that "develop products and services based on Oracle technologies." Additionally, Oracle pledges to provide support for its companies with marketing, distribution, and technical support.

Even underwriters are entering the VC game. Firms such as Morgan Stanley, Goldman Sachs, and Hambrecht & Quist have VC arms. Underwriters benefit for several reasons. First, since it is an early investor, the underwriter will likely see a large rate of return on its investment. Second, it is usually easier to have the company as a client for underwriting services, since there is a pre-existing relationship.

In recent years, there has arisen a new style of venture firms called incubators. These firms invest in companies in the very early stages and become highly involved in the company's growth. In many cases, the start-up will even share offices with the incubator. Examples of incubators include CMGI, which backed Lycos and GeoCities, and idealab!, which backed GoTo.com and Tickets.com.

So how did Akamai do? The offering was priced at $26, and on its first day of trading, the price soared to $145. The company was able to raise $234 million. By the end of the year, the stock hit a high of $345. Unfortunately, when the Nasdaq plunged in April 2000, so did Akamai. In mid-November 2000 the stock was trading at $38.

AUTIDOR

THE PURPOSE OF an auditor in the IPO process is to vouch for the accuracy of a company's financial statements. An analysis ensures that the company's accounting practices are consistent with generally accepted accounting procedures (GAAP). The auditor is required to be independent of the company in order to avoid any conflict of interest.

Auditors will also help the IPO candidate draft the financial reports in compliance with SEC requirements and will issue a "comfort letter" that the underwriter uses for due diligence.

Having an experienced, well-regarded auditor is very important. If the audit is mismanaged, the IPO may be delayed by SEC questions about the financial data.

Another key advantage of having strong auditors is that they can help devise an effective budget and a long-term planning process for the company. These basic tools enable the public company to forecast cash flows, plan for new capital expenditures, control interest costs, and structure a tax-efficient compensation package for managers. The leading IPO auditors are the Big 5 accounting firms: Pricewaterhouse Coopers, Ernst & Young, Arthur Andersen, KPMG, and Deloitte & Touche.

ATTORNEYS

CONDUCTING AN IPO requires a team of attorneys to deal with the many complex regulations for proper state and federal compliance and disclosure. Talented legal counsel is absolutely essential to any IPO. If counsel makes mistakes, the IPO could be a disaster.

The role of the attorneys is to review existing contracts, amend the articles of incorporation and bylaws, develop stock incentive plans, readjust the capital structure, and so on. They will help deal with the officials at the SEC, review the registration documents, and provide advice on what management can and cannot say to the public.

In some cases, a company will, out of loyalty, use the attorneys they have dealt with since inception. Although this will ensure that the attorneys are very familiar with the company's practices, it may also be problematic if counsel does not have the necessary IPO experience.

TOP IPO LAW FIRMS

HERE ARE SOME of the top IPO law firms:
- ◆ Wilson Sonsini Goodrich & Rosati, Palo Alto, California
- ◆ Cooley Godward LLP, Palo Alto, California (main office)
- ◆ Brobeck, Phleger & Harrison, San Francisco, California
- ◆ Hale & Dorr, Boston, Massachusetts
- ◆ Venture Law Group, Menlo Park, California

FINANCIAL PRINTER

IPOS GENERATE A blizzard of paperwork. A prospectus, for example, can easily be 300 to 400 pages long. Depending on the size of the offering, a company may have to send out thousands of prospectuses across the United States and throughout the world. The printing must typically be done on very short notice—in many cases within twenty-four hours. What's more, there can be no typos—the document must be flawless, as the SEC requires.

There are about twenty financial printers that specialize in IPOs and are familiar with the myriad of SEC rules regarding filing format, such as paper, type size and font, colors, and so on. In other words, having your neighborhood copier company do the printing would be a disaster.

Interestingly enough, when *Wired* magazine attempted to go public in 1996, there was so much disagreement between the company and its underwriter (Goldman Sachs) regarding the font style, it should have been a warning sign that the offering was in trouble.

Believe it or not, such seemingly insignificant things can wreck a deal.

PUBLIC RELATIONS FIRMS

PUBLIC RELATIONS FIRMS are crucial in stock offerings. After all, PR is a powerful tool for attracting investors. There are many companies going public these days—all competing for the attention of the press and investors. Without good PR, an IPO can easily be lost in the crowd.

However, as with most things financial, the SEC has certain guidelines regarding public relations. The company cannot disclose anything that varies from the contents of the prospectus. If this rule is violated, the company could suffer serious consequences—such as the SEC terminating the offering. PR firms that specialize in IPO marketing know the rules and know how to get the message out to the right brokers, investors, institutions, analysts, and market makers.

Unfortunately, some companies use PR to cloud the

facts. This type of misleading information is sometimes found in obscure offerings from unknown companies. Therefore, it is wise for investors to be skeptical of information contained in the press releases. After all, some of the facts are bound to be glossed over in the spin. It's better to focus on the facts contained in the prospectus.

TRANSFER AGENT/REGISTRAR

THE ROLE OF the transfer agent is to maintain shareholder information. For example, the transfer agent will hold the name, address, Social Security number, and number of shares purchased for each shareholder. In an IPO it is the transfer agent who handles the physical delivery of stock certificates to those who have indicated interest in purchasing shares. When the stock begins trading, the transfer agent will handle the transfer of stock certificates in every buy-sell transaction.

The registrar, on the other hand, ensures that the correct number of shares are exchanged when there is a buy-sell transaction. The registrar will also keep records of destroyed, canceled, or lost stock certificates.

The company doing the IPO will typically hire an out-

ADVISERS FOR THE JUNIPER IPO

JUNIPER NETWORKS INC. (JNPR), located in Sunnyvale, California, is a leading provider of high-end routers, which efficiently manage Internet data traffic. The company filed its IPO on June 24, 1999. However, in order to get to that point, the firm relied on many top advisers. They included the following:

◆ **Lead underwriter.** Goldman Sachs & Company
◆ **Law firm.** Wilson Sonsini Goodrich & Rosati
◆ **Auditor.** Ernst & Young
◆ **Transfer agent.** Norwest Bank Minnesota
◆ **Venture capitalists.** Kleiner Perkins Caufield & Byers, New Enterprise Associates, Ericsson Business Networks, Northern Telecom Limited, and Crosspoint Venture Partners

side firm, such as a bank, to act as the transfer agent. In most cases, this firm will act as both the transfer agent and the registrar.

UNDERWRITERS

UNDERWRITERS PLAY A pivotal role in executing a successful initial public/offering. The managing underwriters are the investment bankers who run the IPO show. They determine the price of the offering; help draft the prospectus and other filing documents; conduct due diligence; and most important, find investors for the offering.

In many cases, the underwriter will continue to provide services even after the IPO is completed. For example, the underwriter might advise the newly public company on matters such as mergers and acquisitions or debt offerings.

The managing underwriters will also assemble a group of syndicate underwriters. It is the syndicate that helps sell the IPO's stock to the public. The main reason for a syndicate is to share liability—that is, if there is a shareholder's lawsuit, the liability can be dispersed.

It's hard to exaggerate the importance of an under-

SYNDICATE UNDERWRITERS FOR AKAMAI

COMPANY	SHARES
Morgan Stanley & Co. Inc.	3,690,000
Donaldson, Lufkin & Jenrette Securities Corp.	1,845,000
Salomon Smith Barney Inc.	1,845,000
Thomas Weisel Partners LLC	820,000
Adams, Harkness & Hill, Inc.	100,000
Credit Suisse First Boston Corp.	100,000
Dain Rauscher Wessels	100,000
First Union Securities, Inc.	100,000
Hambrecht & Quist LLC	100,000
Edward D. Jones & Co., L.P.	100,000
Charles Schwab & Co., Inc.	100,000
Soundview Technology Group, Inc.	100,000

writer. Having the right one in place can mean the difference between a successful IPO and a failed offering. So before you invest in any IPO, it makes sense to investigate the underwriter. Interestingly enough, the underwriting business is the prime source of revenue for securities firms. For more information on types of underwriters, see Appendix A, on page 248.

This chapter is meant as a general overview to give the reader a sense of the IPO world. The next section goes into greater detail on the IPO process. It is surprising that even many investment professionals do not understand some of the changing intricacies of IPOs. However, to be a successful IPO investor, it is imperative to know how the procedure works.

CHAPTER

The IPO
PROCESS

THIS CHAPTER TAKES a look at the IPO process from the moment when management decides to do an IPO to the time when shares are sold to the public. These are the basic steps that precede an initial public offering:

◆ Due diligence is conducted.

◆ Letter of intent is signed.

◆ Registration statement is drafted and filed with the Securities and Exchange Commission.

◆ The road show begins the marketing.

◆ Investors are solicited.

◆ The company chooses a listed exchange or over-the-counter market.

◆ The offering is finalized.

The IPO process is more complicated than many investors realize. Before examining each step, take a quick look at the descriptions of the legislation that governs IPOs.

LAWS THAT LEGISLATE IPOS

TWO PRIMARY FEDERAL statutes that cover IPOs were legislated during the Great Depression after abuses in the stock market during the 1920s. The Securities and Exchange Commission (SEC) enforces these laws:

♦ **Securities Act of 1933.** This "Truth in Securities" act requires that before any stock is sold to the general public, the securities must be registered with the SEC. The prospectus can contain no material misstatements. Such misstatements can lead the SEC to file civil and criminal sanctions against the company and its underwriters.

♦ **Securities Exchange Act of 1934.** This requires that a registered public company make periodic disclosures. Furthermore, the act has sanctions for violations of unfair market practices, such as insider trading.

In addition to these federal laws, there are also state

laws, called blue-sky laws, regulating IPOs. The name is derived from a nineteenth-century court case in which the judge compared a stock offering to someone selling the blue sky. These laws are important because they dictate the logistics of the IPO process.

DUE DILIGENCE

BEFORE AN IPO can get rolling, underwriters must perform due diligence on the company—an extensive investigation. They visit offices, conduct interviews, analyze the financial statements, scrutinize the accounting procedures, and consult with the auditors. The best underwriters will even talk to customers and suppliers. The purpose of a due diligence investigation is to minimize the legal risk to underwriters, because they are liable for material misstatements in the prospectus, just as the company itself is liable.

If, after due diligence, the underwriters are satisfied with the company's prospects and are interested in orchestrating the offering, a letter of intent will be drafted and signed.

LETTER OF INTENT

A LETTER OF INTENT is an understanding between the company and the underwriter. It sets forth the tentative terms of the relationship, like the percentage of ownership, minimum/maximum amount of money to be raised, counsel for the underwriter, counsel for the company, compensation for the underwriter, and so on. The letter of intent also establishes a range for the offering price of the issue. For example, the price range may be $14 to $18, but over time this price may be adjusted. Since it may take several months to get approval for the offering, it is virtually impossible to determine an exact price for the stock.

A letter of intent is little more than an agreement to agree. It is not a binding contract. A final agreement is not usually signed until the day before or the morning of the offering. The company's responsibility to pay all of the fees for professional services, however, is binding after the letter of intent is signed. Though cancellations are rare, the collapse of an IPO can leave the company with debilitating expenses.

The final underwriting agreement is identical to the letter of intent except for the addition of the final stock price and number of shares to be issued. There will also need to be an agreement among underwriters. This document expresses the number of shares to be allocated among the comanagers and syndicate underwriters and enumerates the compensation breakdown.

Deciding the price of the issue is one of the most complex tasks of an underwriter. The firm will look at factors such as the valuations of prior IPOs in the same sector and the company's stature within its industry. If a company has a proprietary technology or tremendous market share, there may be a premium to the valuation. But ultimately, the pricing tends to be more of an art than a science.

The stock must not be priced too high, which would deter investors. In fact, offerings are typically underpriced to encourage investor participation. When the stock is offered, the price will often make a big jump on the first day. It's not uncommon to see the stock price soar 30 to 40 percent almost immediately.

VeriSign, a company that develops digital IDs for the Internet, did its IPO on January 30, 1998, with the help of the underwriter of Morgan Stanley Dean Witter. Because of huge demand, the price was boosted from $12 to $14 per share. About 3 million shares were offered to the public (about 15 percent of the company), and at the opening, the stock increased to $17. By the end of the day, the stock was up to $25.50, an 82 percent increase. An IPO that sells at a high premium on its first day is called a "hot" IPO.

At one time it was considered an embarrassment to have such a major price increase on the first day, because it meant that the company could have raised much more money, but it's now becoming standard practice to witness these huge premiums.

In some cases there are selfish reasons for underpricing. Planning for a huge premium, for example, makes it easier for underwriters to engage in the questionable practice of spinning. Spinning is a routine by which an underwriter allocates a certain amount of IPO stock to potential clients (usually companies that are headed for IPOs themselves). By spinning lucrative IPOs to potential clients, underwriters are hoping to get the company's business in the future. Spinning, though, has come under heavy criticism and is currently being investigated by the SEC.

For the most part, it is very risky to purchase an IPO on the first day of its offering. There tends to be a frenzy of trading activity and price fluctuation; rationality can go out the window as investors bid on a limited number of shares. It's often safer for individual investors to wait several months and let the dust settle before buying their shares.

DRAFTING THE
REGISTRATION STATEMENT

AFTER THE LETTER of intent has been signed, the registration statement must be drafted and filed. There are two parts to the registration statement: (a) the prospectus and (b) additional information, which includes summaries of the expenses, insurance for officers and directors, the underwriting agreement, and so on.

Drafting the registration is a time-consuming task. The first step in the process is called the "all-hands" meeting, in which all the participants (management, attorneys, underwriters, auditors, and so on) gather to initiate the steps for creating the registration statement and are assigned their specific tasks.

The most important document in a registration statement is the prospectus, because it is the tool that is used to sell the offering to investors. Chapter 4 contains detailed information on reading and understanding an IPO prospectus.

THE TWO TYPES OF REGISTRATION STATEMENTS

◆ **Form S-1.** Any company can use an S-1, but because of its complexity, it is typically used by IPOs raising millions of dollars. The company must disclose three years' balance sheets, statements of income, shareholders' equity, and changes in financial condition. It must also give a detailed description of the business, management compensation, and facilities. Since S-1 filings tend to indicate solid companies, they have more prestige in the industry than SB filings.

◆ **Form SB.** There are two types of SB offerings. **Form SB-1** limits the amount to be raised to $10 million, whereas **Form SB-2** has no limit. An IPO using an SB-1 provides balance sheets for only the past fiscal year; SB-2s, for two years. SB-1s report two years' statements of income, changes in financial condition, and shareholders' equity; SB-2s disclose data from the past three years.

FILING THE
REGISTRATION STATEMENT

WHEN THE REGISTRATION statement is drafted, the company may arrange a prefiling conference with the SEC to allow the company to discuss the details of the offering with regulators. This step can save much time and money, since the SEC officials will provide guidelines on what information the company should disclose.

Next, the company will file the registration statement with the SEC. At the same time, filings will be made with all the states in which the stock will be offered, as well as with the National Association of Securities Dealers (NASD). The NASD analyzes the registration statement to see if the compensation is, in their estimation, fair and equitable.

Its approval of the registration statement can take from six weeks to several months, depending on the workload of the SEC and the complexity of the deal. Before approving the filing, however, the SEC will usually have questions about the offering that are communicated through what are called "comment letters."

THE ROAD SHOW

ALSO KNOWN AS the "dog-and-pony show," the road show allows a company to generate interest from brokerage firms and institutions for the IPO. For approximately two to three weeks, the senior managers visit financial centers, such as San Francisco, New York, and Los Angeles, to give presentations. During the typical breakfast and a slide show, the audience can ask the managers questions.

The general public is not allowed to attend road shows. But Wit Capital, which is an online investment bank, is using Web video technology to give individual investors the opportunity to view these events.

SECURING INVESTORS

BEFORE THE SEC gives its approval, it is not uncommon for the preliminary prospectus to be distributed to potential investors to generate interest. At this stage, the preliminary prospectus is known as a red herring. Some companies choose to wait until after the first round of comment letters before releasing the red herring to investors, in order to reduce the chance of the embarrassment of having to make significant changes in the prospectus.

Regardless of when it's distributed, a red herring always contains the following disclaimer in red ink on the front of the document:

> Information contained herein is subject to completion or amendment. A registration statement relating to these securities has been filed with the SEC. These securities may not be sold nor may offers to buy be accepted prior to the time the registration statement becomes effective. This prospectus shall not constitute an offer to sell or the solicitation of an offer to buy nor shall there be any sale of these securities in any State in which such an offer, solicitation

or sale would be unlawful prior to registration or qualification under the securities laws of any such State.

Yes, this is lawyer mumbo jumbo. However, it is important for investors to note the disclaimer and realize that the information in the prospectus is not yet final and the offering not yet approved.

Members of the underwriting syndicate use the red herring to begin locating investors for the offering. However, before a broker can even talk to a client about an IPO, he must provide the red herring for review. It is the only information that can be provided. If the investor is interested, he or she will sign an indication of interest. This does not constitute a sale, because the price has not yet been established. It is not until the day of the offering that the sale becomes final. Any broker asking for money before the day of the offering is in violation of securities laws.

During the preapproval time, the company is in its "quiet period." As discussed above, the information released to the public must be in accordance with what is in the prospectus. The only other thing that can be published is a *tombstone ad,* as shown below. You will see these

$100,000,000

South Jersey
Gas Company

Medium-Term Note Program

Dealer

First Union Capital Markets

ads in the back of the Marketplace section of the *Wall Street Journal*. A tombstone may contain the company logo, address, the stock price, and the number of shares to be issued. According to SEC rules, the quiet period ends twenty-five days after the stock starts trading.

CHOOSING LISTED EXCHANGES OR OVER-THE-COUNTER MARKETS

BEFORE A COMPANY can issue shares to the public, it must decide in which market the shares will be listed and traded. In most cases, an IPO will be listed on the over-the-counter (OTC) market, which is simply a network of computers. Because many companies are relatively small when they are first public, OTC distribution makes more sense than exchange trading because exchanges have size and volume requirements that most smaller companies can't meet.

The most prestigious listed exchange is the New York Stock Exchange (NYSE). Trading on the NYSE gives a company instant visibility that translates into increased trading volume. The NYSE has a physical trading floor, where brokers buy and sell stock, and 1,300 members. To be listed on the NYSE, a company must meet minimum requirements that include having pretax earnings of $2.5 million, $18 million in assets, 1 million shares outstanding, and 2,000 shareholders.

There are some IPOs that are large enough to be listed on the NYSE. Hertz, for example, did its IPO on the NYSE in April 1997.

There are also four regional stock exchanges, all with physical trading floors: Pacific, Midwest, Philadelphia, and Boston. The companies that do IPOs on these regional exchanges tend to be small and local. Their trading is usually very light.

The over-the-counter market is more of a virtual exchange. The over-the-counter forums include:

◆ **Nasdaq NM** (National Association of Securities Dealers Automated Quotation System National Market). This is the OTC market for top-tier firms. They must have a minimum of $4 million in net assets, $750,000 in net earnings, and 400 shareholders.

Interestingly enough, today even major companies are opting to list on Nasdaq instead of listed exchanges like the NYSE. Nasdaq has gained the reputation as the exchange for high-tech, high-growth companies. The NYSE has a reputation for more traditional businesses—such as banking, insurance, and manufacturing. In fact, even though such companies as Microsoft, Intel, Cisco, Dell, and Oracle could easily list on the NYSE, they prefer to stay on the more hip Nasdaq.

◆ **Nasdaq Small Cap.** This exchange is for companies that cannot meet the requirements for Nasdaq NM. Qualifying factors include 300 shareholders and net assets of $2 million; no net earnings are required. Nasdaq's membership consists of 5,400 companies.

◆ **Pink Sheets.** Penny stocks are traded on the Pink Sheets. (Penny stocks are small, illiquid stocks with very little revenue. They are too risky for most individual investors.) The name is derived from the pink paper on which the quotations for this market are printed. There are about 15,000 companies listed on the Pink Sheets—however, the listing requirements are less rigid than Nasdaq's.

◆ **Bulletin Board.** Bulletin Board provides up-to-date information—i.e., real-time quotes—on Pink Sheets stocks. This is an automated, centralized system on which approximately 6,000 stocks are listed. However, the Bulletin Board and Pink Sheets markets are not stock exchanges. They are quotation services. What's more, both the Bulletin Board and Pink Sheets are loosely regulated. Thus, they can be dangerous for individual investors. Interestingly, some companies try to disguise the fact that they are listed on the Bulletin Board by telling investors they are listed on "the Nasdaq Bulletin Board." Don't be fooled.

FINALIZATION OF THE OFFERING

AN IPO IS READY for prime time when the SEC approval is final, the underwriting agreement is signed, and the price and number of shares are set.

The "effective date" is when SEC approval is granted. After the effective date, the company is allowed to sell its shares to the public. The number of shares and price of the issue are determined on the day of the offering. This final step can be a particularly grueling process for everyone involved.

"I have seen fights over 25¢ between the company and the underwriter," says Larrie Weil, head of the IPO department at Southwest Securities. "Then again, a price difference of 25¢ can amount to $10 million."[1]

Depending on market conditions, the offering price may be set higher or lower than the estimated price range. The printer will then print a final version of the prospectus, which will be sent to all the buyers of the offering.

Once this process is complete, the company is officially public.

IPOs FOR
Investors

PART

I

CHAPTER

Finding the BEST IPO INFORMATION

THE FIRST STEP in any smart investment decision is research. But the reality is that many individuals don't spend nearly enough time investigating the soundness of their potential investments. Instead, they act on rumors or rely on tips from their hair stylist or other questionable "experts." Sure, it is possible to get lucky with this type of advice; the stock might soar—but relying on luck is risky.

So the first lesson for any investor is: Don't buy any IPO strictly on rumors. After all, if you're going to spend $1,000 or $5,000 or even more on a stock, isn't it a good idea to investigate the company?

At the other end of the spectrum there are investors engaging in "analysis paralysis." They think that in order to win on Wall Street you need to have the most complex, state-of-the-art investment strategies. You need to use esoteric investment vehicles, such as derivatives, and calculate extensive mathematical formulas. Thankfully, you can make a lot of money without engaging in these mental gymnastics. It has been shown time after time that good investing has everything to do with common sense—as long as it is based on a foundation of sound facts.

As recently as a few years ago it was difficult to get reliable research on companies. You had to purchase expensive subscription services—which were sent to you in the mail and arrived somewhat dated. But all that's changed. Today, the Internet and even some print publications have more than enough timely information to help you make sound investment decisions, and much of that information is free!

This chapter is designed to help you find the information you need about upcoming IPOs, see what the analysts are saying about their chances, and track their performance. Pay attention when you get to the EDGAR section, where you'll learn how to access information on any IPO—directly from the SEC. There is also a Resources section at the end of this book. It contains a more exhaustive listing of IPO information sources of every stripe, as well as addresses, telephone numbers, and Web sites for the sources described in this chapter.

INFORMATION TO GET YOUR FEET WET

THERE ARE A LOT of great places to read about the comings and goings of IPOs. These publications and Web sites will help you to learn the industry and to feel comfortable with the terminology. We'll describe more advanced IPO investment tools later in this chapter. But first, let's start with some lighter-weight sources of investor information.

THE WALL STREET JOURNAL

THIS IS THE DAILY BIBLE for IPO investors—and just about every other type of investor, too. There are routinely a variety of articles on specific IPOs, plus stories on current trends in the IPO market. The "Heard on the Street" column will occasionally cover hot IPOs, and you will see frequent IPO stories from the *Wall Street Journal* staff writer Randall Smith.

The print version of the *Wall Street Journal* costs $175 per year; the online edition is $59 per year ($29 if you are a subscriber to the printed version). The Web site has the same information as the printed version. In fact, in many cases, the online articles are longer and more up-to-date.

You can also set up your own "Personal *Journal.*" This tool allows you to create a customized section of the *Journal* that will search for articles based on key words and phrases, such as "IPO." It's a very simple yet powerful tool to track IPOs. There is also a portfolio feature, with which you can track stocks. One strategy is to create a hypothetical portfolio of IPOs and track their performance over time. It's a great way to learn about IPOs without actually risking your assets.

Any investor who is interested in investing in IPOs should get accustomed to reading the *Wall Street Journal* and using the tools offered on its Web site (www.wsj.com).

BARRON'S

THIS IS A WEEKLY business and finance newspaper that contains in-depth analysis of companies and stocks. The writers are not afraid to tell it like it is. And *Barron's* arguably has the best inside IPO coverage of any publication available on the newsstand. Every week there is "*Barron's:* Review and Preview," written by *Barron's* staff writer Robin Goldwyn Blumenthal. Keep an eye on that feature for current IPO analysis.

All the content of the printed version is also contained in the online edition. If you want to subscribe, sign up for the online edition of the *Wall Street Journal,* and you'll have access to *Barron's* and also *SmartMoney* Interactive as part of that package.

A one-year subscription to the print edition of *Barron's* is $145 (www.barrons.com).

INTERNET STOCK REPORT

I WRITE A COLUMN for the Internet Stock Report called "IPO Tracker," which comes out several times a week. It includes a look ahead at upcoming IPOs, a detailed profile of an IPO that will soon price, and a look back at how the week's IPOs have done. The site also has an IPO Center that features IPODEX, an IPO index, and Internet IPOWatch!, which lists information on Internet companies that have filed to go public and a ninety-day activity history of Internet companies that have recently gone public. It is worth checking out if you're an IPO watcher, and yes, the information is free (www.internetstockreport.com).

THESTREET.COM

THESTREET.COM IS the creation of the outspoken James J. Cramer, who writes a high-profile investment column for several magazines and also runs a hedge fund. TheStreet.

com is very informative and timely, and articles are posted throughout the day. If anything, it is fun to read. You will find the analyses of IPOs always strong and engaging, and the information is free (www.thestreet.com).

THE MOTLEY FOOL

THE MOTLEY FOOL is a lot like TheStreet.com. Both are exclusively online, well-written and -researched, and much fun to read. The Motley Fool is also completely free. You will see a variety of coverage on companies that are going public (www.fool.com).

THE RED HERRING

THE RED HERRING is both a magazine and an online publication. It covers the high-tech sector. It's a great resource for information about the hottest IPOs and for interviews with the movers and shakers. Plus, there's great industry analysis. A one-year subscription to the print edition is $49, although new subscribers can get their first year for just $29 (www.redherring.com).

OTHER ONLINE RESOURCES

YAHOO!, EXCITE, AND SILICON INVESTOR are other useful Web sites to check out regularly when you are researching IPOs. Yahoo! Finance has a section on IPOs, which has an extensive list of the latest IPO news and events (www.yahoo.com). Excite includes a feature called "IPO Insight" in its money and investing section. There is also an IPO calendar and performance information. However, to access the IPO information on Excite, you must subscribe to the S&P Personal Wealth Service, which costs $9.95 per month or $99.95 per year (www.excite.com). Silicon Investor is linked to an IPO section powered by IPO.com (detailed later in this chapter), all of which can be accessed for free (www.siliconinvestor.com).

IN-DEPTH IPO INFORMATION

THE INFORMATION AGE has put an end to good information on IPOs being either unavailable or proprietary. Here are some of the best places to do in-depth research on specific companies and upcoming IPOs. If you're serious about investing in IPOs, you should familiarize yourself with one or several of these resources. As you'll see, most of these databases and news services are online, which allows constant updating and real-time information.

BLOOMBERG

BLOOMBERG FINANCIAL MARKETS has added an IPO center to its comprehensive and free financial Web site. It covers all of the following:

◆ The latest IPO listings
◆ IPO headlines from Bloomberg News
◆ IPO Focus column
◆ The Bloomberg IPO Index, which is a capitalization-weighted index that tracks the performance of IPOs during their first year of trading (www.bloomberg.com).
◆ A list of new mutual funds
◆ Bloomberg IPO Index Movers, which lists the ten best- and worst-performing members of the Bloomberg IPO Index.

IPO CENTRAL

A JOINT VENTURE between Hoover's and EDGAR Online, this is one of the best IPO sites on the Web. Hoover's, based in Austin, collects research on more than 12,000 U.S. and foreign companies. Even private companies are covered. EDGAR Online is discussed later in this chapter.

IPO Central contains an incredible amount of useful information that is updated daily:

◆ **Latest Filings.** A list of the companies that have filed S-1s or SB-2s during the past week.
◆ **IPOs in Registration.** A complete listing of those companies that have filed a registration statement but have yet to

start trading (it takes about four to six weeks until the shares are offered).

◆ **This Week's Scheduled Pricing.** A list of companies expected to start trading in the next week.

◆ **Aftermarket Performance.** A review of how well individual IPOs have done after trading has started.

◆ **Withdrawals and Postponements.** A listing of companies that have delayed or completely withdrawn the offering.

◆ **Find an IPO.** A search feature for an IPO based on name, key word, underwriter, state, or metro area.

◆ **IPO Directory.** A comprehensive list of companies that have filed for an IPO on or after May 6, 1996, searchable by date or company name.

◆ **IPO Close-Up.** A weekly commentary on a current IPO.

◆ **Featured IPO.** A Hoover's Company Profile feature that must be purchased. However, every week there is an additional featured IPO that has a free link to a Hoover's Profile.

◆ **Beginner's Guide.** A great resource of articles and Web sites about the IPO world.

◆ **Front-Page Links.** Six to seven weekly links to IPO articles on the front page of IPO Central.

Yes, everything above is free. However, if you want even more detailed information, such as real-time SEC documents, financial reports, market data, and industry comparisons, then you can subscribe for $14.95 per month or currently only $109.95 per year (www.ipocentral.com).

IPO MONITOR

IPO MONITOR PROVIDES a comprehensive set of services for IPO information. One of its best features is its e-mail notifications, which alert subscribers to the following:

◆ **New Filings.** Daily e-mail regarding companies that have filed a registration statement.

◆ **Going Public.** An e-mail list sent every Monday of companies that are expected to price for the current week.

◆ **New Pricing.** An e-mail that shows which companies have been priced and are being actively traded. It is normally sent in the morning, giving you a head start to buy the IPO in the aftermarket.

◆ **Aftermarket Performance.** A weekly list of companies indicating how they have performed since their offerings.

Although you can obtain the same information by going to IPO Monitor's Web site, the e-mail notification is extremely useful. What's more, IPO Monitor has an extensive data research sheet on the Web site for any company that registers to go public. You can search for companies based on name, industry, and underwriter. The data sheet includes such things as contact information, industry classification, underwriters, description of the business, number of shares offered, expected price range, names of senior managers, major shareholders, balance sheets, and income statements.

This all-inclusive information comes with a price tag. The subscription fee is $29 per month or $290 per year (www.ipomonitor.com).

IPO DATA SYSTEMS

IPO DATA SYSTEMS has a comprehensive database of IPO financial filings that extends back to January 1994. There are more than 2,500 detailed company profiles (the 2000 profiles are free). These profiles contain more than 200 items—including balance sheet, income statement, use of proceeds, principal shareholders, and contact information.

The company also will sell you a copy of every IPO prospectus for all domestic and foreign offerings since January 1997 in electronic (MicrosoftWord) format. One year's worth of IPO prospectuses costs $150, two years' worth costs $250, and three years' worth costs $300.

For a subscription fee of $15 per month, $30 per quarter, or $100 per year, you get the following:

◆ IPO filings for the current week
◆ Every IPO pricing for the week
◆ List of upcoming IPOs
◆ Search of the database based on a variety of criteria

(such as key words, industry, and so on)

◆ List of IPO performance year-to-date

◆ List of the top underwriters based on number of deals, total dollar amount of the offerings, and percentage gains

There are also free sections on the site. You can read commentaries from various IPO analysts or peruse a list of direct public offerings (companies that are doing their own offerings without the assistance of an underwriter) (www.ipodata.com).

ALERT-IPO

ALERT-IPO IS ONE of the cheapest IPO subscription services. For $34.95 per year you receive weekly summaries via e-mail that detail which companies have filed for IPOs during the past week. Every day you receive reports on each company that has filed within the past twenty-four to forty-eight hours. You can access the latest pricings, filings, postponements, withdrawals, and IPO news. There are also some free areas on the site. For example, you can click to a section that provides a weekly summary report of recent filings, and you can access online prospectuses for more than 4,000 IPO filings, although real-time filings are available only by subscription (www. ostman.com/alert-ipo).

CBS MARKETWATCH-DBCC

THIS IS A LEADING provider of real-time financial information and commentary. The IPOWatch news section includes the following:

◆ **IPO Daily Report.** Brief descriptions of the latest companies going public.

◆ **IPOnder.** An in-depth commentary on an upcoming IPO, which I write.

◆ **IPO First Words.** Interviews with investment bankers, executives, and analysts who are involved in the IPO market, written by Steve Gelsi.

◆ **This Week's IPOs.** A list of companies going public for the current week.

◆ **IPO Pick of the Week.** An IPO investment that looks good according to the analysts at Renaissance Capital, by David Menlow.

◆ **IPO Basics.** This is a four-part article by Darren Chervitz that describes the IPO process.

◆ **IPO Headlines.** Current IPO-related stories.

◆ **Discuss: IPO Talk.** A message board to discuss companies that are about to trade or have recently traded.

The site is a tremendous resource, and all information and articles are free (www.cbs.marketwatch.com).

THE IPO SPOTLIGHT

THE IPO SPOTLIGHT is a subscription publication that can be either e-mailed to you for $30 per month or faxed for $40 per month. The service provides basic IPO information, such as the expected date of issuance, size of the deal, lead underwriters, and so on.

What makes the service unique is that it provides recommendations on which IPOs to buy. But be wary of some of the claims it makes: "get in on the IPOs with the great profit potential, without the research and prospectus study normally required." This is probably not a good idea—you want to make sure you understand exactly what you are investing in (www.ipospotlight.com).

IPO MAVEN

MANISH SHAH, A widely quoted authority of the IPO market, manages the IPO Maven site. It provides the following:

◆ **CEO Talk.** Interviews with the CEOs of public companies.

◆ **Stock Watch.** A list of IPOs that look promising.

◆ **Market Summary.** Several paragraphs describing each of the latest IPOs.

◆ **Company Stories.** In-depth analyses of various companies (although not all of them are IPOs).

◆ **Q & A.** Articles that describe the ABCs of IPOs.

◆ **Calendars.** A list of upcoming IPOs and recent pricings, as well as companies that have postponed or withdrawn their offerings.

◆ **IPO Performance.** Overviews of sectors, showing which are the hottest and which are the worst.

◆ **IPO Corner.** Two or more IPO updates daily and articles on IPO aftermarket recaps.

◆ **IPO Research.** A snapshot look at various IPOs.

◆ **IPO Alert.** E-mail notifications of companies that registered to initiate an IPO, pricings, and top stock gainers/losers (www.ipomaven.com).

IPO.COM

IPO.COM FEATURES THE LATEST IPO news and an IPO calendar that lists upcoming pricings. An IPO event log includes withdrawals, first-day closings, the price range in which companies are expected to file their IPOs, and recent filings and pricings. There is a quiet-period calendar; a lockup-period calendar; an aftermarket report; and listings of IPOs by underwriter, by accountant, and by law firm. IPO.com also has information on venture capital firms and an IPO glossary. You can use their "EDGAR-search" to see the filings of each company's prospectus.

Registering for IPO.com is free; all you have to do is complete a short registration form. You will receive a newsletter and can sign up for e-mail alerts, although you may want to choose your categories wisely, since you could end up receiving more than 100 e-mails a week if you sign up for all of the options (www.ipo.com).

IPO FINANCIAL NETWORK

IPOFN ONLINE PROVIDES upcoming pricings, free daily e-mail updates, brief company profiles, *IPO Frontline* Newsletter Commentary reprints, and an IPO glossary. The service also is currently offering a pre-opening snapshot, which tracks every Nasdaq IPO from when it shows its orders through the beginning of trading. The pre-opening snapshot is currently $99 for a three-month subscription.

IPO Frontline is a twice-a-month print publication that includes a market commentary, stock capsules, a corporate pre-IPO investors listing, an IPO calendar pipeline, underwriter participation, complete company profile data, the IPO heat index, and a listing that tracks the performance of the top twelve underwriters on deals within the last twelve months. A one-year subscription costs $850, for which you also receive free access to the pre-opening snapshot.

IPOfn Telephone Network gives you access to IPO information over your telephone. The New Issues Hotline offers a new issue recap and pricing update, IPO ranking update, calendar update, evaluations by individual underwriter, daily changes in evaluations, secondary ranking update, selling group information, buy/sell recommendations, and underwriter locations. All this comes for $3 a minute. The Top 15 Hotline features the top five IPOs for the next week, the top five IPOs for the following week, and the top five IPOs for the week after that. For each stock the following categories of information are provided: Participating Underwriters, Hot Listed Since, Projected Opening Bidside Premium, Percent Opening Premium, and Selling Group Information. A subscription to the Top 15 Hotline costs $250 for thirteen weeks.

IPOfn Fax Packages include the Money Managers/ Traders Package (the daily report subscription rate is $1,000 per month, and the weekend report subscription rate is $250 per month/per report when you subscribe to the daily reports); Action Track Packages (which cost either $600 per month or $900 per month for the secondary action track); the After-Market Performance Analysis Package (level one costs $1,000 per month, and level two costs $2,000 per month); and the Syndicate Package (which costs $95 per week, with a four-week minimum) (www.ipofinancial.com).

EDGAR RESOURCES

THE SEC'S EDGAR

THE FIRST PLACE I VISIT to investigate any IPO is EDGAR, which stands for Electronic Data Gathering Analysis and Retrieval. This huge online database of financial filings was developed by the SEC.

Any company that files a registration for an S-1, SB-1, or SB-2 offering must present an electronic version of the filing, which is placed in the EDGAR database. In other words, by going to the EDGAR site, you can get the full version of any company's prospectus. And as we will see in the next chapter, it is in the prospectus that you will find much of the necessary information to help you make investment decisions. But you cannot retrieve EDGAR filings in real time; there is a twenty-four-to-forty-eight-hour delay.

EDGAR is not very pretty graphically. The filings you download are in raw form, and you will often see spaces in the lines of text. But then again, the information is free. And you get everything you need to examine an initial public offering (www.sec.gov).

You can search the database in the following ways:

◆ **Quick Forms Lookup.** If you already know the name of the company, then use this feature. The search name must be twenty characters or fewer, however, so this feature may be less useful if you're researching mutual funds.

◆ **Search the EDGAR Archives.** You use such key words as "and," "not," and "adj." So if you want to find documents that have filings for both Microsoft and Intel, you specify "Show me the documents for Microsoft *and* Intel." If you want documents from either Microsoft or Intel, then use "or." If you want to exclude something from the search, then use "not." For example: "Search all documents for Microsoft *not* Intel." As for "adj," this stands for adjacent and means that two words must always be together. So if you specify a search for "cordless *adj* telephone," then you will get those documents that have only "cordless telephone." An asterisk (∗) tells the search engine to match the characters that precede the ∗ and to ignore any trailing characters. For example, if you specify "Micro∗", you will get matches for Microsoft, Microsystems, and so on.

◆ **Special Purpose Search.** This allows you to search certain types of filings, such as quarterly reports, proxies, or prospectuses.

THERE ARE SOME OTHER useful sites and tools that use EDGAR's information in a more aesthetically pleasing format. These include the following:

FreeEDGAR

THIS SITE HAS several features that are worth exploring. You can search filings by company name, ticker, SIC code, location, zip code, or date filed. Also, check out the Watchlist feature, which allows you to create a custom list of companies that you're interested in tracking. FreeEDGAR will then notify you via e-mail when any company on your list submits an electronic filing.

So far, FreeEDGAR is the only company offering free, unlimited access to real-time corporate data filed with the Securities and Exchange Commission (www.freeedgar.com).

IPO EXPRESS

IPO EXPRESS IS A SITE powered by EDGAR Online. It contains current IPO headlines, latest pricings, upcoming pricings, and latest filings. You can gain access to a quiet-period calendar, a lockup-period calendar, a listing of bull/bear rankings on upcoming IPOs, international IPOs (alphabetically by country), postponements, and withdrawals. The site also lists IPOs by underwriter, by industry, and by state. IPO Express has a performance table for IPOs (www.ipoexpress.com).

EDGAR ONLINE

LIKE FREEEDGAR, EDGAR Online provides real-time access to financial filings from the SEC. There is a subscription cost, but also many benefits:

◆ You can download the filings into MicrosoftWord or other programs that support RTF (Rich Text Format).

◆ Real-time notification of filings via e-mail, based on a watch list.

◆ Use of toll-free customer support and e-mail support (in fact, you get this free even if you are not a subscriber).

◆ Extensive searching capabilities of the database (company name, ticker symbol, form type, sector, industry, geographic location, and date range).

◆ Access to other value-added financial content, such as PC Quote, BigCharts, Hoover's, and Zack's.

◆ A database extending back to 1994.

◆ EDGAR Online People is a great resource that allows the user to search financial statements to obtain background information—such as compensation—on officers and significant owners of public companies. No other site has this type of research capability.

◆ E-mail notification for new IPOs as they are filed, priced, postponed, or withdrawn (an additional $3 a month over your subscription fee).

Subscriptions start at $9.95 per month; the fee is based on how many filings you download. As for the free services, you get all the benefits listed above, except the data is not real time. However, for most investors, you do not need real-time data. Even if the data are delayed several days, it should not make a difference, because it takes four to six weeks for the IPO to occur (www.edgar-online.com).

OTHER IPO INFORMATION RESOURCES

NEWSLETTERS

THERE ARE THOUSANDS of investment newsletters, many costing upwards of $500 per year. But the choices are less confusing for the IPO investor, since there are only a few newsletters that cover this sector. Here is one to check out:

◆ *New Issues.* The editor, Norman Fosback, has a vast understanding of the IPO market. There are articles about the general conditions of the IPO market, as well as profiles of individual companies. When you subscribe, you get a free book, written by Fosback, called *Stock Market Logic.* The newsletter is issued every month and also has e-mail alerts; $179 per year (800-442-9000).

CHAT ROOMS/DISCUSSION GROUPS

THESE CAN BE VERY worthwhile for investors who want expert answers to questions. But you should also be skeptical of what you read on message boards—there is no real way of knowing who is posting a message. True, it could be from someone who understands the investment. But the respondent may also be a former investor who has an ax to grind, or the CEO, who wants to pump up the stock.

Disregard messages like "This stock will go up 600 percent in two months" or "This stock will definitely go bust."

In fact, a variety of phony IPOs have been orchestrated by using discussion groups. Be skeptical of information that seems too good to be true. Check out the discussion boards listed in this book's Resources section.

COMPANY WEB SITES

IF YOU WANT INFORMATION on a specific company, why not go right to the source? Looking at the Web site of the company doing the IPO can be a tremendous resource. You will see press releases, bios on the management, a customer/partner list, testimonials, case studies, and a lot of other detailed content. But as you might suspect, this isn't the place to look for unbiased, hard-hitting data. Expect to find mostly public relations–approved news.

YOUR BROKER

A FINAL SOURCE OF information on IPOs is your stockbroker. Many brokerage firms have access to research that is not accessible to the general public. And if you're lucky, your broker may have heard the buzz on the Street regarding an upcoming IPO and be willing to share information with you.

INFORMATION TO STAY AWAY FROM

NOT ALL INFORMATION is good information. Here are some IPO information sources to avoid:

◆ **Spam.** Spam is unsolicited e-mail. It's become a huge business, primarily because it is so easy and cost-effective to send simultaneous messages to millions of people. Some look very personalized, and others look as if they were sent to you accidentally. But keep in mind that spam is never accidental. It's a marketing tool, not objective information. Some spam will offer you the "opportunity" to buy into IPOs or investments. It's a good idea to stay away.

◆ **Unsolicited mail.** If you sign up for magazines or online journals, you are likely to be put on a variety of mailing lists. In order to promote their IPOs, small companies will purchase these lists and send out very professional, glossy marketing materials. In most cases, a company has hired a PR firm that knows how to hide the negative and hype the positive. These may actually be "pump and dump" offerings—when a company's officers issue large amounts of stock to brokers, creating the illusion that the stock has done a successful offering, as the price soars. The brokers, in turn, will dump the stock on clients.

As with spam, buyer beware.

◆ **Cold calls.** Cold calls are a key part of the brokerage business. It's called "dialing for dollars." These brokers are playing a numbers game. The more calls they make, the more people will put their money into the "hot" investments they are selling. By far, cold calling is the most cost-effective means of marketing. To be successful, there needs to be only a 1 to 2 percent closure rate.

In most instances, you simply don't want to buy what cold callers are selling. Remember this: If it were such a hot investment, they wouldn't be selling it unsolicited over the telephone. Don't ever buy IPO shares over the telephone.

But cold callers can be very convincing. They spend hours every day making the same calls, using the same script. If you want to reduce the number of calls you receive, ask the broker to put you on the Don't Call list, or write a letter to the compliance officer of the firm.

Now that we've explored where to look and where not to look for the latest IPOs and their fundamentals, let's turn to the one information resource all investors need to read before buying any IPO: the prospectus.

CHAPTER

Making
SENSE OF THE
PROSPECTUS

OST OF THE specifics you need to evaluate an IPO are contained in its prospectus. The company is required by law to disclose all material information—the good, the bad, and oftentimes, the ugly. It's all in there.

There are several ways to get a copy of the prospectus. The easiest way, as discussed in Chapter 3, is to download the document free from Hoover's IPO Central site or from the SEC's Web site. Your other option is to call the lead underwriter and request that a copy of the preliminary prospectus, or "red herring," be mailed to you, or you can call the company itself and request a copy. Prospectuses are not hard to come by; reading them, on the other hand, is another matter altogether.

Reading a prospectus is not like browsing through your favorite entertainment variety magazine; a prospectus is long, full of jargon, and laden with charts and graphs. And here's the worst part—it's written by a lawyer.

But as daunting as this document might appear, you don't need an advanced degree to understand it. Remember: the prospectus is crucial, but you don't have to read all of it. There are a variety of sections that have very little bearing on the IPO investment. For example, many prospectuses contain the lease agreement for the company's facilities. This is something you can skip. This chapter focuses exclusively on the sections of the prospectus that are most important to investors.

As you continue reading prospectuses, the process will get easier and faster. But like anything else, it takes practice. As you read through this chapter, it's a good idea to have a sample prospectus (from www.edgar-online.com) in front of you to look at as the pertinent sections are described here.

GOOD NEWS FOR INVESTORS

THE SEC ADOPTED what are called "plain-English" rules for drafting prospectuses. These rules require that the cover pages, the summary, and the risk factors section be easy to understand, for obvious reasons. Basically, the issuer must comply with these three rules:

1 short sentences with concrete, everyday language

2 active, rather than passive, voice

3 bulleted lists for complex information; absolutely no legal jargon; and no multiple negatives.

To help promote plain-English rules, the SEC vows that it will delay approval for registration statements and prospectuses that do not comply. This happy development makes it much easier to analyze an IPO prospectus.

A prospectus usually has between twenty and thirty sections. These are the most common ones investors should expect to see:

1 Front Page

2 Prospectus Summary

3 The Company

4 Summary Consolidated Financial Data

5 Risk Factors

6 Use of Proceeds

7 Dividend Policy

8 Dilution

9 Capitalization

10 Selected Quarterly Financial Results

11 Liquidity and Capital Resources

12 Management's Discussion and Analysis of Financial Condition and Results of Operations

13 Business

14 Management

15 Certain Transactions

16 Principal Stockholders

17 Description of Capital Stock

18 Shares Eligible for Future Sale
19 Certain United States Federal Tax Considerations for Non-U.S. Holders of Common Stock
20 Underwriters
21 Legal Matters
22 Experts
23 Additional Information
24 Index to Consolidated Financial Statements

The remainder of this chapter explains the portions of the prospectus that IPO investors need to understand and to focus on.

FRONT PAGE

THE FIRST SECTION of the prospectus is called the Front Page. And yes, it all fits on one page. This is where you'll find some basic reference information on the company and, more specifically, on the offering. You'll see the type of offering it is, such as an S-1 or SB-2. (These offering types are described on page 37 in Chapter 2.) You will also find the address of the company, the names of the managing underwriters, and the exchange that the stock is expected to list on. As you read through the Front Page, you'll see that it contains a table called the Calculation of Registration Fee. It looks like the one in the box below, which is from the prospectus of the February 2000 IPO of webMethods, Inc. (WEBM).

The Calculation of Registration Fee table contains important information: the estimated share price of the offering. In webMethods's case, the price is listed as $35. But when a company first files its prospectus, the initial

CALCULATION OF REGISTRATION FEE			
	PRICE TO PUBLIC	UNDERWRITING DISCOUNTS AND COMMISSIONS	PROCEEDS TO WEBMETHODS
Per share	$35	$2.45	$32.55
TOTAL	$143,500,000	$10,045,000	$133,455,000

public offering price is usually stated as a range, because it may take a few months until the stock is eligible to be sold to the public. For example, in late January 2000, the company filed a prospectus with the SEC that had a proposed price range of $11 to $13. Within a few weeks, the company filed another prospectus that changed the price range to $28 to $30. Such a rapid increase in the price range indicates there is huge demand with an IPO. And this was definitely the case. On its first day of trading, the stock soared to $212. ✔

You will also see footnotes listed on the Front Page. One common footnote describes the *over-allotment option*. This allows the underwriter to issue additional shares during the IPO, an option that is exercised if there is heavy demand for the offering. In the case of the webMethods offering the underwriter has the option of purchasing 615,000 more shares than the maximum being offered. The underwriters have thirty days to exercise this option.

As you read further down the Front Page of the prospectus, you will see how many shares the founders and officers are selling. In this offering, the managers did not sell any of their shares. However, if you see an IPO in which the founders and officers are selling 30 percent or more of the amount being offered, it may mean that they are bailing out: in other words, these individuals may not believe in the long-term viability of their company but want to get as much cash as possible on the day of the offering. This should be a red flag for IPO investors.

STANDARD SEC DISCLAIMER

THESE SECURITIES HAVE NOT been approved or disapproved by the Securities and Exchange Commission or any state securities commission nor has the Securities and Exchange Commission or any state securities commission passed upon the accuracy or adequacy of this prospectus. Any representation to the contrary is a criminal offense.

It's important to remember that all prospectuses contain the disclaimer shown at left on the Front Page. In other words, the SEC will not advise whether the offering is a good or bad investment; it's not in the business of recommending stocks. It is up to you to decide if the investment has potential. The SEC simply maintains that the company has complied with the securities laws, such as disclosing the necessary information in the right format.

QUALIFICATION REQUIREMENTS

IN SOME PROSPECTUSES, but not all, you'll see a section just before the Prospectus Summary that's known as Qualification Requirements.

Investors beware. Qualification Requirements mean that a state or the SEC deems the offering to be risky and that only high net worth individuals may participate. Such a restriction can have a severely negative impact on an offering. If you see Qualification Requirements, you'll know that an IPO is a particularly high-risk investment.

THE COMPANY

THE COMPANY SECTION runs from five to ten paragraphs or longer. In it you will find a description of the company and its products and services. For example, webMethods's IPO prospectus stated, "We are a leading provider of infrastructure software and services that allow companies to achieve business-to-business integration, or B2Bi. B2Bi software is a new category of software that enables companies to work more closely with their customers, suppliers, and business partners through the real-time exchange of information and transactions."

The Company section may also contain various surveys or research reports illustrating the market size for the company's products and its target audience. This section is a *must-read* for investors. It's always important to understand the business a company is in before investing in its IPO.

In the last paragraph of the Company section, you will see the state in which the company is incorporated. In most cases, it will be Delaware. But take note that if the company is incorporated in an offshore haven, such as the Bahamas, investors need to be very wary. The reason for such offshore incorporations is to make it difficult for the SEC to enforce its laws against the company.

RISK FACTORS

THE FACT THAT A PROSPECTUS lists risks doesn't, in itself, mean that the IPO is a bad investment. In fact, a prospectus that fails to list any risks would probably never receive SEC approval. After all, by nature investments are never entirely free from uncertainty. Chapter 5 goes into greater detail on some of the more significant risk factors investors should watch for. Here are some of them in brief:

◆ **History of loan default.** This shows that the company will probably go bankrupt unless it raises money from an IPO. The IPO, in other words, is really an act of desperation.

◆ **Negative gross margins.** This means that the company is not likely to make money for quite some time, if ever.

◆ **Recent transition to a new business.** This can mean that the company has lost its focus and does not have clear goals for the future or that it's moving into a business that it originally was not set up to pursue.

◆ **Legal proceedings.** Lawsuits are difficult to quantify. What's more, lawsuits can drain resources and divert the attention of management away from its business operations.

◆ **Prior unsuccessful offering.** This means that the company had trouble convincing investors to invest in the IPO.

◆ **Inexperienced management team.** Running a public company requires an experienced management team. Managers who are not qualified will cause major problems for the company.

◆ **Product concentration.** Relying on a single product is risky. If the customer base dries up or the product becomes outdated, the impact can be substantial.

◆ **Low-priced stocks.** Penny-stock IPOs are highly risky. Many of these companies have inexperienced management teams, unproved business models, and little capital with which to expand their business.

USE OF PROCEEDS

AS THE NAME IMPLIES, the Use of Proceeds section indicates exactly what a company intends to do with the money it raises in the IPO. In many cases, this section is vague. However, investors should look for certain things. For example, you will often see an estimation of how long the company will survive on the infusion of IPO capital. In most cases, it is more than one year—but keep in mind that this is only a guess. Many things can happen to a company, good and bad. If more than 50 percent of the proceeds from an IPO are earmarked for outstanding debts, chances are that the company has dismal growth prospects.

DIVIDEND POLICY

FOR THE MOST PART companies that do IPOs don't pay dividends. The reason is that most of them will invest the IPO capital back into their operations in order to accelerate growth.

But there are some industries that do pay dividends. Real estate investment trusts (REITs), for example, are required by law to distribute at least 95 percent of their annual taxable income to shareholders in the form of dividends. Other industries that pay dividends include banks and insurance companies.

On occasion, you will see a major dividend distribution when the IPO is initiated. This is always a one-time event with the purpose of providing liquidity for the owners of the company, who, in most cases, founded the business years ago and are using the opportunity to cash in. It is understood that the company founders should reap the benefit of their efforts and vision, but sometimes that compensation can go too far.

DILUTION

DILUTION IS THE DIFFERENCE between what existing shareholders (founders) and new shareholders (investors) will pay for shares. The existing shareholders usually pay a much lower price for the stock than IPO investors do. Dilution is common in all IPOs. However, sometimes it can be excessive.

A reasonable number to look for in the prospectus is 60 to 70 percent dilution. Anything much higher than that can signal a problem for investors.

SELECTED QUARTERLY FINANCIAL RESULTS

A CHART SHOWING the income statement data broken down by quarters can indicate developing company trends. However, keep in mind that some of the quarterly data can be misleading. For example, a bad quarter may be the result of a cyclical factor and not an indication of the deterioration of the company. So if you are looking at fourth-quarter results, compare them to the fourth quarter of the prior year instead of to other quarters. Quarter-to-quarter results are the most accurate. And try to read the meaning between the numbers. If you see a dramatic drop or increase, make it your business to know the reason behind it.

LIQUIDITY AND CAPITAL RESOURCES

AS THE OLD SAYING GOES, "Cash is king." Without it, you have no company. "This is one of the first things I look at," says Mark Spitzer, president of FreeEDGAR. "I want to see where the company is getting its money and how it is spending it."[2] The Liquidity and Capital Resources section shows how much a company is spending—and on what areas of the business—as well as how much money is in the bank.

BUSINESS

THE BUSINESS SECTION is a comprehensive description of the company, including a succinct summary of the busi-

ACCOUNTING STANDARDS

WHEN READING THE FINANCIAL DATA, you will see the acronym *GAAP*, which stands for generally accepted accounting principles. GAAP rules are the standard principles that accountants abide by when preparing accounting statements. These standards are derived from an organization called the Financial Accounting Standards Board (FASB).

ness, size of the market, company products and services, a description of R&D, the number of employees, and a list of top customers. You'll also read about marketing initiatives and office space.

MANAGEMENT

THIS SECTION LISTS the senior managers of the company and the board members. Each will be described in a one-paragraph résumé. As indicated earlier in this chapter, look for management that has prior experience running public companies. Be careful of companies that have a senior manager who currently works for or used to be part of the investment bank that is managing the IPO. Such management may be more concerned about engaging in financial shenanigans to line their pockets than in running the company for the long term. At the very least, there is the potential for conflicts of interest.

Also be cautious of companies that have senior managers who are related to each other. If the CFO is the twenty-four-year-old son of the founder/CEO, the company could run into trouble.

CERTAIN TRANSACTIONS

THIS SECTION SHOWS the history of the financing of the company, including the involvement of angel investors and venture capitalists. Look for companies that have angels with strong industry experience. And look for VCs with good track records.

On occasion, you will see some evidence of conflicts of interest. For example, the company may have lent money to some of the senior officers. Or the company may be doing business with a firm owned by a senior manager. Thus, the company may not get the best deal, which could hurt shareholder value.

SHARES ELIGIBLE FOR FUTURE SALE

SIX MONTHS AFTER a successful IPO, you may see the stock suddenly fall, say 10 or 20 percent, without any apparent reason. The cause of such a sell-off may be that the lockup period has expired and company insiders are cashing in some of their stake.

A lockup provision, disclosed in this section of the prospectus, gives control of a company's stock to the underwriters for a limited period of time. Essentially, venture capitalists, founders, and senior executives are restricted from selling their stock for about 120 to 180 days to prevent major selling pressure.

When the lockup period expires, however, the holders of the stock may want to start selling, especially if the stock has increased a great deal and appears to be overvalued. Investors should be aware of the lockup expiration date and realize that they may see some shares changing hands and some price movement.

INDEX TO CONSOLIDATED FINANCIAL STATEMENTS

THIS LAST SECTION of the prospectus includes the full financial statements of the company. You don't need to get your calculator recharged right this second, but for those readers who are mathematically inclined, Appendix B, on page 250, contains some handy analysis techniques.

However, we will take a look now at how financial statements are structured. First, let's go to the income statement, which shows the company's sales (revenues) and expenses over a period of time. The difference between these two numbers is called *Income Before Income Taxes.* After you subtract the taxes, the remaining amount is called net income—that is, profit.

INCOME STATEMENT

THIS IS WHAT you'll see on the income statement:

◆ **Revenues.** This includes all the money the company has made. These sales are adjusted for any discounts given and for returns.

◆ **Cost of Goods Sold (COGS).** COGS is the total of financial resources spent to purchase and manufacture the inventory to be sold to customers. COGS is applicable only to product companies. If the company sells services, it will have Cost of Services.

◆ **Operating Expenses.** These include Research and Development, Sales and Marketing, and General and Administrative.

◆ **General and Administrative.** These costs are for salaries for executives and sales personnel; support services; and professional services fees, such as for legal work.

◆ **Revenues or Gains.** These are items that are not within the normal, continuing operations of the company, such as when a company decides to sell a subsidiary.

◆ **Other Expenses or Losses.** These are expenses or losses that are not within the normal, continuing operations of the company. Again, this is a one-time transaction.

◆ **Pretax Income from Continuing Operations.** This is the difference between the Operating Net Income and the other revenues and expenses.

◆ **Income Taxes.** Discloses taxes paid. If a company has losses, it will not have to pay income taxes.

◆ **Net Income.** This is the pretax income minus income taxes.

BALANCE SHEET

NEXT YOU WILL SEE balance sheet information. Essentially, a balance sheet lists company assets, liabilities, and equity. Assets are listed by their historical cost; market-value appreciation is not accounted. For example, suppose a company purchased real estate for $1 million. Five years later, the real estate might be worth $3 million. The asset will still be listed on the balance sheet at $1 million.

The following are the most common asset items on a balance sheet (they are usually listed in order of liquidity):

◆ **Current assets.** These are short-term and can be converted into cash within one year. Examples include:

—*Cash.* This is money in a bank account.

—*Marketable securities.* Stocks, bonds, and other securities.

—*Accounts receivable.* This includes the amount of money that customers owe the company. Often, you will see an item called *Allowance for Doubtful Accounts,* which is an estimate of how much money the company believes it will be unable to collect from customers.

—*Inventories.* These include the work in process, raw materials, and merchandise used in the manufacturing and selling operations.

—*Prepaid expenses.* These are expenses for services that a company has paid for but has yet to receive. Examples: prepaid rent, prepaid insurance.

◆ **Noncurrent assets.** These are assets that can be converted into cash after at least one year. Examples include:

—*Long-term investments.* Stocks, bonds, and other securities that will be held for the long term. However, to be classified as long-term, the company must have a significant stake in the stock or bond (usually at least 20 percent).

—*Property, plant, and equipment.* Long-term assets such as the land, machinery, tools, and buildings used in the normal course of business. You will typically see another item called *Accumulated Depreciation.* Depreciation is a method a company uses to expense long-term assets.

—*Natural resources.* Resources such as oil, gas, minerals, or timber that can be extracted from the ground. When these resources are removed, the company will deduct the value of the natural resources item by a process called depletion.

—*Intangible assets.* These are nonphysical, long-term assets. Examples include copyrights, patents, franchises, trademarks, trade names, and goodwill. Goodwill is the excess of the cost of an acquired company over its book value.

LIABILITIES INCLUDE both current and noncurrent items:
◆ **Current liabilities.** Debts that must be paid within one year. Examples include:

—*Accounts payable.* Money a company owes its suppliers.

—*Current maturities of long-term debt.* Expenses related to long-term debt. For example, suppose a company has a mortgage for $10 million that is payable over ten years. The current year's interest payment will be listed in this category.

—*Unearned revenues.* Revenues that have been collected in advance, such as magazine subscription revenues.

—*Accrued expenses.* Money owed for taxes, payrolls, and other expenses.

◆ **Noncurrent liabilities.** These are debts with payments extending beyond one year.

—*Contingent liabilities.* Money a company may potentially owe for things like pending litigation. The company will estimate the amount of this liability.

—*Deferred income taxes.* A difference between the numbers on the company's financial statements and the numbers reported on the income tax statement. The method to calculate a company's financial statements and income taxes are usually different. Thus, this difference represents a liability to the U.S. government.

—*Leases.* A capital lease is reported on the balance sheet. That is, the company is essentially getting complete ownership of the property through the lease. However, if this is not the case, then the company has an operating lease, which is not reported on the balance sheet. Look for it in the footnotes.

—*Long-term debt.* Mortgages and notes.

◆ **Equity.** Equity is the difference between the total assets and liabilities. So, if the company has $30 million in assets and $20 million in liabilities, the equity is $10 million. Thus, this $10 million is the ownership interest in the company.

These are some components of equity:

—*Capital stock.* The par value of the stock issued. This value is stated on the stock certificate and is an arbitrary value; that is, a nominal amount (such as 0.001¢). The stock is either common stock or preferred stock.

—*Paid-in capital.* The excess of the capital stock.

—*Retained earnings.* The profits that have been reinvested back into the company. However, it is more typical for a company to have negative retained earnings (since early-stage companies usually lose money). This is known as an *accumulated deficit.*

—*Treasury stock.* Stock that a company has bought back. Since an IPO has never traded on the market, the Treasury Stock item does not apply. Convertible Preferred Stock shows the amount of money investors have put into the company.

CONCLUSION

CONGRATULATIONS TO THE READER. You have just made your way through the most important parts of an IPO prospectus. Remember: the prospectus is an investor's best friend. It contains most of the information you need to make your investment decision. Chapter 5 goes into more detail on some of the risk factors you might see in the prospectus. Knowing what the risks are is important; realizing what they might mean to your investments is vital.

CHAPTER

Risk
FACTORS

Y LAW, A COMPANY must clearly list in its prospectus all potential risk factors for investors: company situations or industry conditions that might negatively impact the future of the business and the stock price. All investments have risks. What's important, though, is to be able to identify those that might cause trouble for the IPO. This chapter describes some of the risk factors you might spot in an IPO prospectus that warrant further consideration.

INEXPERIENCED MANAGEMENT TEAM

IT IS CRITICAL FOR a company to have a management team that knows how to deal with business complexities that might arise. A recently hired team is one risk factor warranting careful consideration.

Peritus Software Services (PTUS) is a company that develops software and provides services to improve the productivity and quality of the information technology systems of companies. In 1996, Peritus released a product called the AutoEnhancer/2000 that dealt with the Year 2000 problem.

The company grew from $7.8 million in sales in 1994 to $19.2 million in 1996, and the number of employees increased from 130 to 229. But with this growth came some problems worth noting. In 1997, when Peritus initiated an IPO, members of the company's senior management had been with the company less than one year and had limited experience in managing public companies. The top-line underwriter, NationsBanc Montgomery Securities, handled the May 1997 IPO. Shares were issued at $16 per share, raising $44.8 million. In November 2000, Peritus Software was selling at about 9¢ per share.

Be wary of twenty-something management teams. An example is theglobe.com (TGLO), which provides free Web sites to consumers. While students at Cornell

University, Todd Krizelman and Stephen Paternot started the company in the fall of 1994. Krizelman earned a bachelor's degree in biology and Paternot earned degrees in business and computer science.

The company went public in November 1998, at which time both founders were twenty-four years old and co-CEOs of the company. The stock shot up from $9 to $63.50, and the IPO raised $31 million. But after much turmoil and difficulty executing the business model, the stock was trading below $1 per share in November 2000.

Inexperience within the management team isn't the only reason the stock price is flat, but it certainly has a bearing on the performance of any company.

LEGAL PROCEEDINGS

ANOTHER RISK FACTOR worth investigating is serious litigation pending against the company. The problem with litigation is that it is difficult to quantify. After all, it is almost impossible to know how a jury will decide a case, or how much it will award a company in damages. What's more, a protracted lawsuit can divert a company's attention and resources away from its focus.

Here are two interesting examples:

◆ **Jenna Lane (JLNY).** Founded in 1995, the company designs, manufactures, and markets sportswear for women. Several people associated with management had run-ins with the law. The president and co-CEO was convicted in state court for larceny. In addition to this, Stanley Kaplan, who helped promote the stock offering of Jenna Lane, signed a consent decree with the SEC for securities violations. All of this was disclosed in the prospectus. Jenna Lane went public in March 1997, raising $6.1 million. The offering price was $10.13. In November 2000 the stock was selling for 2¢.

◆ **eMachines (EEEE).** The company sells low-priced PC systems. Unfortunately, before its IPO the company was party to a variety of lawsuits. In July 1999 Compaq Computer filed suit against eMachines for alleged infringement on thirteen patents held by Compaq. Then in August 1999 Apple Computer filed a complaint against eMachines for alleged unfair and unauthorized use of the design and trade dress of the iMac computer. eMachines eventually went public in March 2000 at $9 per share, raising $180 million. But on its first day of trading, the stock closed at $8.25. At the time of this writing in mid-November 2000 the stock was trading at 75¢.

Also, be wary of any disclosures of legal problems involving the underwriter. In certain states, an underwriter having been banned from financial activities can definitely stunt the offering.

MARKET AND CUSTOMER BASE

AN IDEAL CANDIDATE for IPO investment is a company with a potentially large, fast-growing market. This sounds obvious, but not all IPO candidates are lucky enough or are designed to have diverse product offerings.

Product concentration can be a major problem for young businesses. A company may have only a few products, sometimes just one. And if such a company's singular product hits a sales slump, it can lead to overall underperformance for the company and its stock.

Reliance on a small number of customers, similar to product concentration, limits potential for growth and chances to recover in an evolving, competitive marketplace. Be careful of a company that sells its products to only a few customers.

An example is ASD Group Inc. (ASDG). This company provides contract manufacturing and engineering services to original equipment manufacturers, such as GE and IBM. However, 71 percent of net sales are derived from four customers. In December 1996, two of the company's largest customers temporarily reduced shipment levels. The company went public at $5.75 in May 1997, raising about $6 million. In mid-November 2000 the stock was selling at 27¢.

BUSINESS MODEL

WITH THE RAPID GROWTH of the Internet, many new companies have gone public. However, most of these new companies were based on new business models, and it is not uncommon for this fact to be mentioned in a company's prospectus as a risk factor. If you see this, it is important to think very critically about the company—developing a new business model is extremely difficult. However, when it is successful the results can be great, as was the case with eBay (EBAY), which developed the person-to-person online auction market.

One example of a new model that failed is drkoop.com (KOOP). The site provides useful medical content for consumers. In the company's prospectus, there was the following risk factor: "Consumers and the health care industry may not accept our product offerings." The company openly admitted that up to that point, consumers had relied on health care professionals as their main source of health care information. Of course, drkoop.com thought this would change. What's more, the company bet that other companies would want to advertise on drkoop.com, which had plans to provide e-commerce opportunities to consumers.

The company went public in June 1999. The offering price was $9 and reached a high of $45.75. Unfortunately, drkoop.com was unable to attract enough revenues, continued to suffer losses, and began to run out of money. At the time of this writing, the stock was selling for about 70¢.

NEGATIVE GROSS MARGINS

THINK TWICE BEFORE INVESTING in any company that has negative gross margins. It's possible that such a company will never be profitable.

Rockwell Medical Technologies (RMTI) is an example of this scenario. The company develops hemodialysis concentrates and dialysis kits. Unfortunately, the company's cost structure has resulted in huge losses. Since its inception, the company has had a gross margin deficit of

$391,119, primarily the result of the company's massive transportation costs—it has its own trucking operations.

As Rockwell's prospectus states: "There can be no assurance that the company will ever operate at a profit." This is a very serious statement to see in the Risk Factors section of any prospectus.

Rockwell's stock was offered at $4 per share. In mid-November 2000 the stock was selling at under $2. And since the IPO, the company has continued to incur negative gross margins.

Another example is Buy.com, which has a reputation as a deep discounter. According to the company's prospectus, "Because we sell a substantial portion of our products at very competitive prices, we have extremely low and sometimes negative gross margins on our product sales." In 1999, Buy.com incurred losses of $130.2 million.

The company went public in February 2000 at $13, raising $209 million. On its first day of trading the stock hit $25.50. In mid-November 2000 the stock was trading at around $1.50.

OPERATIONAL SYSTEMS

A COMPANY CAN HAVE great products, but if the operational systems are antiquated, there will likely be disaster. That is, running a fast-growing business requires a strong infrastructure that can handle increasing amounts of volume.

One company that faced operational difficulties is Value America (VUSA), an online retailer. The problems were disclosed in the Risk Factors section of the prospectus: "Our rapid growth to date has challenged our management's ability to ensure that our financial systems keep pace with such growth." This was a determination based on an audit from the company's accounting firm. The report concluded that there was a "significant deficiency" in the systems. For example, the systems were unable to determine product shipment dates and order statuses on a timely basis. This became even more foreboding as the company approached the Christmas season.

Value America had its IPO in March 1999. The offering price was $23 and the stock surged to $45. In mid-November 2000 the stock was selling for 5¢.

GOING CONCERN

IN MOST CASES, when an auditor analyzes a company's books, there are no surprises. But sometimes there will be a so-called going-concern determination. Basically this means that the company is expected to run out of cash soon. Of course, with an IPO a company will get an infusion of cash, which often means there will then be no going-concern problem—at least for awhile.

If you see a going-concern determination in a company's prospectus, it is probably a good idea to avoid the stock. Such companies typically continue to have financial problems.

For example, drkoop.com (mentioned earlier in this chapter) had a going-concern determination. True, the company was able to raise $84 million in its IPO, but drkoop.com aggressively spent the money (such as on expensive deals with AOL), and the business model had problems. On April 25, 2000, the company's auditor once again gave a going-concern determination.

B2Bstores.com (BTBC) also had a going-concern determination. The site allows businesses to transact with each other using the Net. At the time of its IPO, the company had "nominal" revenues and losses of $2.9 million. The IPO, which was priced at $10, raised only $28 million, and in mid-November 2000 the stock was selling for $1.69.

LIMITED HISTORY OF PROFITABLE OPERATIONS

IT TAKES TIME to build profitable operations. In its early stages, a company will spend a lot of money developing its infrastructure, products, and market share. However, over time, the company should be able to reach critical mass and achieve profitability. In fact, raising capital through an IPO should help accelerate the process of reaching critical mass, but it takes time.

Many high-tech companies, for example, have big losses in their early years. This was the case with Internet service provider America Online (AOL), which spent millions building its infrastructure and customer base. Once this was complete, though, the company became a dominant player in the high-tech world. In fact, AOL became big enough to purchase Time-Warner in early 2000.

So just because a company is unprofitable in the short term does not mean the IPO will fail. Rather, the key factor is that the expected future growth rate should be high.

However, be wary of those companies that describe long-term losses—over ten years or more. This is a strong indication that the business will never be profitable.

SkyMall (SKYM) is an example of an IPO with long-term losses. If you've flown on an airline, you've seen SkyMall's catalogs, which are located in the front pockets of each passenger seat. The catalog is chock-full of premium (that is, expensive) goods from Disney and the Sharper Image. In fact, SkyMall has about 70 percent of the market for domestic passengers, or 960,000 passengers each day.

Before going public the company had impressive revenue growth. From 1991 to 1995, sales grew from $5.4 million to $43.1 million, while sales per passenger increased from $0.038 to $0.084. Despite this growth, the company was unable to generate any profits. The gross margins were small because of high distribution and printing costs and low markups. In fact, the company had accumulated losses of $32.4 million.

SkyMall went public in December 1996. The amount raised was $16 million, and the offering price was $8 per share. Since then, the company has been a dismal performer. In mid-November 2000 the stock was trading at about $2. By reading the Risk Factors, it would have been easy to spot this company's long string of losses.

You may also find a company that has a long history of erratic earnings. This is the case with Celerity Systems (CLTY). The company designs, develops, integrates, and installs interactive video services hardware and software, as well as CD-ROM software products for business applications.

Founded in 1993, Celerity Systems incurred losses of $264,000 the first year. In 1994, the company lost $30,000, and in 1995, it generated profits of $9,900. Then, in 1996, the company had a huge loss—$5.5 million. For the first six months of 1997, the company had losses of $3.8 million. The Risk Factors in the company's IPO prospectus indicated that the company reserved about $570,000 for uncollectable accounts receivable and $673,000 for uncompleted contracts. Also disclosed were problems with a major customer, which was reluctant to pay its bills.

Even with this questionable earnings pattern, Hampshire Securities took the company public in November 1997 at $7.50 per share, raising $15 million. At the time of this writing in November 2000 the stock was selling for 17¢.

UNSUCCESSFUL PRIOR PUBLIC OFFERING

ON OCCASION, AN IPO will fail. A company will file its registration statement to go public but will then pull the offering from the market, usually because there is little demand for the stock. (Investors do not lose money in such a situation, because the stock has not been sold.) Perhaps the market environment is bad, or the company is slipping. That same company may, after a year or two, try again to complete an IPO. Be careful with companies that try repeat IPOs; they can be very risky investments.

One example is ThermaCell Technologies (VCLL). The company originally tried a "best efforts" offering in 1996, attempting to sell a minimum of 833,333 shares at $6 per share. But the IPO failed because the company was unable to generate enough demand for the stock (investors were skeptical of the company's prospects). All investor funds had to be returned. Because of the expenses of the failed offering, the company had to close its Florida sales office, vacate its executive offices, reduce significantly its marketing plans, and lay off employees. The company also defaulted on its $505,000 bridge loan.

Despite these problems, the company was able to return to the capital markets and do an IPO again in 1997, raising $5.5 million. The offering price was $4. In mid-November 2000 the stock was selling for 66¢.

The original failed attempt of the IPO was not the only reason for the latter failure. There were other reasons, such as poor operating performance of the company. However, the fact that the company had a failed attempt at an IPO was a strong indication that serious problems existed.✓

COMPETITION

COMPETITION IS MENTIONED in every prospectus. It is the nature of business as we know it. In fact, the presence of competition can be positive, because it indicates that there is a market for the company's products or services.

However, sometimes competition can be extremely fierce, particularly in fast-paced industries like technology. In any case, it's a potential risk factor that investors need to be aware of. Reading the Competition section of the prospectus can give investors a very good idea of the various players in the industry that are vying for market share.

An interesting example is TheStreet.com (TSCM), which is a comprehensive financial Web site including news, commentary, information, and community features such as online chats.

If you read TheStreet.com's prospectus for its May 1999 IPO, you would clearly see risks of competition stated. In fact, the company called the competitive landscape "intense." Examples sited included CBS MarketWatch, the *Wall Street Journal* Interactive Edition, and the Motley Fool. What's more, with the exception of the *Wall Street Journal* Interactive Edition, these competitors did not charge for their content, whereas TheStreet.com did.

This did not deter TheStreet.com from having a strong performance on its opening. In May 1999, the company launched its IPO at $19. On its first day of trading, the stock hit $60. But since then, the competition has been intense indeed, and the company's stock price suffered a major fall. In mid-November 2000 the stock was trading for about $3, and the company has created a new strategy to offer both free and subscription-based Web sites.

RISK OF LOW-PRICED STOCK

IF A STOCK is offered at below $5 per share, then according to SEC regulations it is considered a "penny stock." Penny stocks, as noted in Chapter 2, are extremely risky and, for the most part, not appropriate for individual investors. Their chances for long-term success are questionable.

One example of a penny stock is BusyBox.com (BUSY). The company, which is a distributor of photos and film over the Net, had a small underwriter on its IPO: Barron Chase Securities. The BusyBox.com IPO was priced at $5 per share, raising about $12.5 million. On its first day of trading, the stock was up 11.25 percent. However, on the second day, the stock plunged to $4.63.

DEFAULT ON OUTSTANDING INDEBTEDNESS

IT IS COMMON for a company to borrow money prior to an IPO. But default on such a debt is an indication that the company suffers from poor cash management. Since a default has a material impact on the company, it is mentioned in the prospectus.

One such company is Marine Management Systems (MMSY). The company develops, markets, and sells software for the communications systems of commercial ships in the international maritime industry. Marine has twenty-seven years of experience in the industry and a large customer base of 1,500 installations. Despite this, Marine was spending huge amounts of cash before its IPO. By the time of its offering in May 1997, the company had a negative working capital deficit of $1.8 million.

The company had to borrow large sums of money to feed the spending, a debt that was backed by the assets of the company. Thus, in the event of a default, the bank would have legal title to the company. But when the company did violate certain loan covenants, it was able to obtain a waiver for the violations.

When you see a company with problems in its debt structure, be extremely careful. It is likely to be an investor time bomb. Marine went public at $5 per share, raising $7 million. In mid-November 2000 the stock was selling at 2¢.

RECENT TRANSITION TO A NEW BUSINESS MODEL

IBM - failed ?
Apple - ?
2018

IT CAN BE SCARY when a company decides to get into a new business—especially within, say, a year or so of its IPO. This makes it difficult to analyze the business, since its prior history is not a good guide to the future. What's more, it is never easy to completely change the direction of a business. Such a process is fraught with risks, for the company and for its investors.

One such example is Qualix Group. The company was originally a distributor, value-added reseller, and publisher of client/server software products. The company then, in 1993, entered the quality-assurance business, introducing a product called QualixHA for the Unix operating system. By 1996, the company took another turn by merging with Octopus Technologies. Now the company develops remote data mirroring products for the Windows NT operating system. Perhaps this partly explains why the company accumulated $6.5 million in losses since its founding in 1990. It went public in February 1997. The offering was priced at $8.50. The stock was sold to Legato (LGTO) for $4 per share.

THESE ARE JUST SOME of the risk factors you'll come across while reading the IPO prospectus. There are other legal, financial, industry, and business risks that also come into play with any investment. The severity of many of these risks depends largely upon the nature of the company and how that specific risk will affect it in the future. If a prospectus is full of seemingly serious risk factors, reconsider the investment, or at least educate yourself further on the risks that are listed.

CHAPTER

6

IPO
INVESTMENT
STRATEGIES

ALL GREAT INVESTORS have philosophies that direct their trading. Warren Buffett, for example, looks for stocks that have strong brand names, substantial market share, and top-notch managements; the famous Peter Lynch's philosophy is similar. William Nasgovitz, manager of the Heartland Small-Cap Contrarian Fund, chooses small, domestic stocks that he believes are undervalued. This chapter will describe a variety of common IPO investment strategies. First we'll examine some simple, commonsense ways to get started in IPOs, then we'll cover some more-sophisticated strategies, often better left to the pros.

BASIC STRATEGIES FOR INVESTORS

NEIGHBORHOOD INVESTING

IN SOME CASES, a great IPO might be happening right in your own backyard. Local companies make tempting investment opportunities because you'll have firsthand knowledge about the business and easy access to research. Perhaps you're even a customer who knows the management personally.

At the very least, close proximity to a company that's going public allows you the opportunity to visit the company's operations and make a firsthand evaluation of its environment. When you visit its offices, learn as much as you can about its products and staff. For instance:

◆ Do the employees look busy and content?

◆ Is the product good quality? Would you use it? *Lynch*

◆ Are the facilities organized and clean?

While you're there, it is also a good idea to talk to the employees. Get their feedback on what they like about their company. In fact, you may even get easier access to shares in the offering if you get to know some of the people who work there. Visiting the company personally won't provide all the answers you need to invest in an IPO, but it will give you a head start.

Another great source of information on regional companies is the local newspaper. You will typically find in-depth business and feature coverage of local companies, and you should even look at the classified ads to see if the company is hiring.

Perhaps one of the best examples of backyard investing is Wal-Mart. The company is now the nation's largest retailer and has made millionaires of thousands of residents of its hometown, Bentonville, Arkansas. Another example is Home Depot, which went public in 1984 with only thirty-one stores. Yes, this company, too, made many people millionaires in its hometown, Atlanta.

INVEST IN WHAT YOU KNOW

IT'S A GOOD IDEA to invest in the industries that you understand best. If you have insight into the construction business—perhaps because you're a builder or contractor—then chances are you have as much insight into industry trends and performance as the analysts. And you're in a great position to more easily determine the upside of companies in that field.

In other words, you should consider your own profession and how it will help you invest in IPOs. If you're a banker and understand the dynamics of the financial services industry, it makes sense to look at finance company IPOs. If you work in Silicon Valley, you have a lot of IPOs to choose from.

You can also use your knowledge as a consumer. If you are an avid book buyer, chances are that you wish you had invested in Amazon.com. If you want to invest in a restaurant IPO, make sure that you dine at that chain. If you are considering an investment in an Internet company, make sure you spend time on its Web site.

Use the knowledge of business you've gained over the years to spot the IPOs with the most potential. Although this is only one of many screens, it's one that everyone can start with.

STUDY MUTUAL FUND HOLDINGS

AS WE'LL DISCUSS in Chapter 12, a variety of mutual funds buy large amounts of IPO shares. One simple strategy for individual investors is to examine the top holdings of such funds. If particular IPOs are good enough for portfolio managers, they might make sense in your personal portfolio, too. There's no telling what ideas you can glean from some of the experts. However, this doesn't exonerate you from engaging in the usual research on the IPOs you discover. After all, even portfolio managers pick lemons.

LOOK FOR VENTURE-BACKED IPOS

VENTURE CAPITALISTS (VCS) are paid big dollars to find the Next Big Thing. And the relationship between VCs and the companies they back is one in which all parties benefit. In addition to providing capital, VCs can help start-ups find top-caliber management, form strategic alliances, and offer operational expertise. So before investing in an IPO, see if there are top VCs behind the deal. If

ANALYSTS' COVERAGE OF IPOS

EVEN IF AN ANALYST does not have an underwriting relationship with the company, you should still remember to be cautious for these reasons:

1 Brokers make their money by getting clients to buy stock.

2 Analysts like high-growth IPOs the most. But high growth may not be what you, as an investor, are looking for (because high growth often comes with high risk).

3 Analysts sometimes give "buy" recommendations for the wrong reason—to give them better access to the company.

4 Analysts are inclined to give "buy" recommendations in hopes of getting the company as a future client for investment banking services. In fact, it is not uncommon for an analyst to get a referral fee for bringing in investment banking clients.

so, there is a good chance the IPO will be big.

One example of a successful VC-backed IPO is Juniper Networks (JNPR), a leading developer of sophisticated router technology for the telecom infrastructure. Juniper Networks was able to attract such all-star backers as Kleiner Perkins, Benchmark Capital, Crosspoint Venture Partners, and New Enterprise Associates. There were also key strategic investors such as Ericsson and Nortel.

The Juniper IPO was in April 2000 at $34 per share. A $10,000 investment would be worth $97,500 at the time of this writing.

RESEARCH THE MANAGEMENT TEAM

RUNNING A SUCCESSFUL public company is no easy task, and there are many examples of failed IPOs. To increase your odds of success, it is critical to focus on those IPOs with seasoned management teams—a good sign of the potential future success of a company.

Commerce One Inc. (CMRC) shows how a successful management team can result in a great IPO. The company develops software solutions for business-to-business applications, and CEO Mark Hoffman was the cofounder and CEO of Sybase Inc. Charles Donchess, the vice president of marketing, was the president of marketing and business development at Aurum Software, a leader in sales information software. Mark Biestman, the vice president of worldwide sales, was formerly the vice president of western U.S. sales for Netscape (he also held top positions at Oracle). Kirby Coryell, the vice president of operations, was the vice president of manufacturing of NEC Technologies. Jay Tenenbaum, the chief scientist, was the chief scientist of VEO Systems. He was also the founder of CommerceNet, the industry association for Net commerce. Clearly, this is a big-name team with a lot of experience and knowledge.

Commerce One went public in April 1999 at $21 per share. In November 2000 a $10,000 investment would have been worth $52,200.

INVESTIGATE THE MARKET'S POTENTIAL

SUCCESSFUL IPOS need to be in billion-dollar market-places. If not, the IPO will experience a slowing of its growth rates. Thus, stay away from companies that are in niches where the marketplace is small and limiting.

One company that capitalized on a market with huge potential is Sonus Networks Inc. (SONS). The company develops technology that allows for the efficient transfer of voice data over the existing telecom infrastructure. The technology also maintains superior voice quality and reliability. With these kinds of credentials, the young company was able to sign up impressive customers such as Global Crossing and Williams Communications.

How big is the market? Well, according to the Synergy Research Group, voice-over Internet technologies are expected to reach about $19 billion by 2003. To put this in perspective, the market was zero in 1999.

The Sonus Networks IPO was held in March 2000 at $23. In August 2000 the stock reached a high of $93. A $10,000 investment would have been worth about $40,500.

WATCH WHAT THE ANALYSTS SAY

AFTER A COMPANY goes public, you might notice that several brokerage firms place "buy" recommendations on the stock. It is a good idea to call those brokerage firms to request these reports. Although you shouldn't base your investment decisions solely on this coverage, it's a valuable source of free research.

Keep in mind, too, that in many cases the underwriter will have its own staff of analysts who publish recommendations, too. You can bet that the underwriting firm will have a "buy" on the stock, but it's still worth reviewing the firm's data. And if an analyst who was involved with the offering comes out with a negative recommendation on the stock, this is a serious indication that the company is in trouble.

The bottom line is that it's very useful to review Wall Street's analysis of an IPO, but it's also important to maintain a healthy skepticism regarding analysts' "buy" recommendations.

BUY ON THE OPENING OR WAIT FOR THE LOCKUP TO EXPIRE?

IF YOU ARE allocated IPO stock at the offering price and it is a hot issue, then it makes sense to participate. A hot issue is an IPO that increases in value immediately upon the effective date of the offering. So, investors holding stock at the opening price have made money immediately.

To spot a hot IPO, look for the following factors:

1 Several days before the IPO, the underwriter increases the price and the number of shares for the offering.

2 Brokers indicate that there are no more shares available.

3 You've heard a good deal of buzz in the press about the IPO.

Buying an IPO at the offering price can mean a very quick profit for investors if their shares are sold quickly. When investors do this, it is known as *flipping*. Underwriters, however, do not look kindly on flipping, because it causes price volatility. In fact, they sometimes penalize investors who flip by not offering them shares in a future IPO.

If you are not allocated shares at the opening price of an IPO, the smartest thing to do is to wait.

Steve Harmon, who was featured in *SmartMoney* magazine as a rising star in technology investing, says, "IPOs are very speculative. And with so much demand on the first day, the price may not immediately be indicative of the company's 'intrinsic' valuation but rather 'instant demand' from buyers. And we all know what happens when demand exceeds supply—inflated prices."[3]

In many cases, an IPO will come back to its offering price at some point in its trading life. The main reason for this is that when a company goes public, there is tremendous excitement. As a result of the hype, the stock will usually jump a great deal. For example, when Broadcast.com went public in July 1998, the stock rose 248 percent on the first day. Investors were excited about the company's Internet video technology. But as time went by, the hype subsided, and so did the stock price.

Unfortunately, there is no scientific formula for buying into an IPO. But here is one sensible approach: wait six months from the effective date before you buy your shares. This is about the time that the lockup period expires (as explained in Chapter 4), which means that the officers and founders of the company will be selling shares. This puts undue pressure on the stock, so you may have an opportunity to get it at a very good price.

ADVANCED INVESTMENT STRATEGIES

SHORT SELLING

ALTHOUGH IT SOUNDS almost un-American, you can make money when a stock falls in value by short selling.

Are you a bear in this bull market? And are you a very sophisticated investor? Then short selling might be an ideal strategy for you.

In a short sell, you first sell the stock in hopes that it will fall. Once the stock is lower, you will buy it back. That is, the buy/sell process is reversed. How do you sell a stock first? Basically, you borrow the shares from your broker and then, later, purchase them in the open market and return the shares to the broker.

Over the years, short selling has become quite controversial. Perhaps the most notorious short seller of all time was the legendary trader Jesse Livermore, who became known as the "King of the Bears." He sold short Union Pacific Railroad stock one day before the San Francisco earthquake of 1906 and made a killing in the process.

Then there was Joseph Kennedy, who purportedly made millions short selling RCA stock (as well as others) just before the 1929 stock market crash. Add to the list the nefarious Albert Wiggan, the president of Chase Bank, who sold short the stock of his own company during 1929 and made $4 million.

SHORT SELLING

A FAMOUS EXAMPLE of short selling takes us back to the debunked carpet-cleaning company ZZZZ Best, founded in November 1985. The founder of the company, Barry Minkow, was in his early twenties. In 1987, the Feshbach brothers, investors who specialized in selling short, began to spot some peculiarities with the company. First, ZZZZ Best announced an extraordinary $8 million contract for carpet cleaning of two buildings in Sacramento. After some research, however, the Feshbach brothers determined that the largest carpet-cleaning contract to date was a mere $3.5 million awarded for cleaning the carpets at the MGM Grand and Las Vegas Hilton. Therefore, the $8 million announcement from Minkow looked like a sham.

The Feshbach brothers took the false contract as a sign that the company was in trouble, so they aggressively shorted the stock—and in the end made a fortune.

ZZZZ Best filed for bankruptcy soon after, and Minkow was eventually sentenced to twenty-five years for securities fraud. It turned out that ZZZZ Best had no revenues at all but was instead a money-laundering scheme.

You don't have to uncover criminal fraud to short a stock; however, you should have a good reason to believe the stock price is about to drop in value.

With this kind of history, short selling has attained a negative connotation. In fact, you will see occasional statements from CEOs denouncing short sellers as irresponsible speculators.

Clearly, this is a strategy best reserved for sophisticated investors. Short selling is actually common in professional money management circles. Famous investors such as George Soros and Michael Steinhardt have popularized the approach. It's a strategy used by many hedge fund managers. However, it's certainly not the right approach for everyone.

That said, the IPO market is ripe for short selling. This is how short selling works for the IPO investor: Suppose a company does an IPO and the stock soars from $10 to $20 on the first day of trading. Also suppose that you have reason to believe the price is highly overvalued and the stock will collapse. Your next step is to short sell, perhaps, 1,000 shares of the stock at $20. That is, you borrow 1,000 shares from your broker and then sell the stock. This will net you $20,000, which will then be kept in an escrow account. However, this is not free. You will have to put up 50 percent of the $20,000 in a margin account. If the stock increases in value, you are required to put up more margin.

What's more, if you sell stock short on the NYSE, AMEX, or Nasdaq, you must make the transaction on an "uptick"; that is, the stock must have increased in value. This is to help prevent undue sales pressure on the stock.

According to the short-sale agreement with any firm, you will need eventually to return the 1,000 shares to the brokerage firm. Let's suppose the stock does collapse to $5. You will then buy 1,000 shares for $5,000 and return the shares to the brokerage, thus netting a $15,000 profit. This is called *covering your short position.*

But what if the stock does not fall, and instead soars to $50. You will need to spend $50,000 to buy back your stock in order to cover your short position. Suppose the stock goes to $90 or $150. In fact, there is really no limit to how much money you can lose in a short sale. It is no surprise that many investors have gone bankrupt from short selling.

As you can see, short selling can be very risky, especially in an offering, because IPO stock can soar to great heights. For example, Onsale.com went public at $6 per share and then quickly fell to $3. Suppose you shorted the stock at $6 but did not cover it at $3. The stock then soared to $32. That would have cost you $260,000 if you had sold 10,000 shares.

If you decide to short sell stock, don't do so merely because a stock has increased or decreased substantially in value. Rather, you must do in-depth analysis of the company and determine a concrete reason to think that the price is about to collapse.

Factors to consider before selling short include:

◆ Significant selling of shares by the company officers and founders

◆ Continually deteriorating profit margins

◆ Escalating debt levels

◆ Fierce competition

◆ Inexperienced underwriter

◆ Prior violations of securities laws by the company managers

◆ Inexperienced managers

◆ Going-concern audit

◆ Expiration of the lockup period

◆ Developmental stage of the company

◆ Few market makers in the stock

◆ Major break in the stock price

◆ Excessive trading volume, such as at least twice the daily average

BUYING ON MARGIN

MARGIN (ALSO CALLED *buying on margin*) is when you purchase a stock with money that's borrowed from a broker. It should be noted that buying IPOs on margin only magnifies the risk that comes with the investment.

In fact, one of the reasons for the famous stock market crash of 1929 was the widespread use of margin (which at the time was unlimited and unregulated). It wiped out many wealthy investors of the day. Although margin accounts have been fairly lucrative during bull markets, they become very dangerous in bear markets.

For the most part, the interest rates on margin loans are very competitive (and much better than most credit cards). But keep in mind: this interest can slowly eat away at your portfolio.

For example, suppose you have a $100,000 portfolio of stocks. You can borrow another $100,000 on margin and buy 10,000 shares of the Onsale.com IPO at $10 each. In five months, if the stock skyrockets to $20, you will have made another $100,000.

But let's suppose the stock falls to $2 per share. Your portfolio of Onsale.com is now worth $20,000. However, all brokerage firms have a minimum maintenance margin of 25 percent to 30 percent of the original amount borrowed—in this case $25,000 to $30,000. Since the current value of the portfolio is below the minimum maintenance margin, you will have a margin call. This means the broker will require you to put up more cash or securities to increase the portfolio to meet the minimum maintenance margin, or the stock in the portfolio will be sold off. Buying IPOs on margin is very tempting, but just like short selling, it can be extremely dangerous.

CONCLUSION

PERHAPS THE BEST piece of advice to take away from this chapter, and this book, is to avoid getting caught up in the hype that often comes with an IPO. It is easy to be lured by the potential for huge gains. But patience is the key. Do your research, study the fundamentals, and wait for the hype to subside. In the end, you should get better value.

IMPORTANT IPO
Sectors

CHAPTER

Technology
IPOs

THE FIRST THING that usually pops into people's minds when they think of IPOs is high-tech companies. This is probably due to the tremendous success in the past few years of the IPOs that have blown through this market. Some serious money has been made in high-tech stocks—the sector that is primarily fueling the U.S. economy.

The world economy is going through an epoch of change comparable to the Industrial Revolution. But instead of wealth being generated by coal, iron, steel, oil, and railroads, the new economy is founded on things on a smaller scale: software, microchips, cell phones, and faxes.

Gordon Moore, a cofounder of Intel, introduced a concept known as Moore's Law that explains the tremendous growth in high tech: the cost of making a semiconductor drops 50 percent every eighteen months. This is why today we can buy a 600-megahertz computer for less than $1,000.

Moore's Law has an exponential effect on the high-tech industry. For example, as computers multiply, software companies generate a bigger base of customers. It took Microsoft only twenty years to become the second-biggest company in the world. As the number of computer sales increases, so does the number of users who have access to the Internet, which helps online companies such as Yahoo! and Amazon.com.

What's more, non-high-tech companies also benefit. They can increase business efficiency and production by buying low-priced computers.

Despite the frantic growth in high tech, the industry is still in its early stages. While there are 240 million personal computers in the world, this number is expected to explode to 2.4 billion by 2010. Furthermore, many of these users will also be using the Internet.

It's important to realize, though, that not every investment in a high-tech company is a good one. Here are some general factors to look for to spot the right high-tech companies and their IPOs:

◆ **Continuing research and development.** R&D is absolutely crucial in high-tech growth. Although large expenditures reduce current earnings, over the long term, R&D can result in tremendous gains. This has been a major factor in the continued growth of such Goliaths as Microsoft, Intel, and Cisco. Intel, for example, spends close to $2 billion annually on R&D.

There are, too, some technology companies that do not need to spend as much money on R&D; such is the case with PC makers, such as Dell and Gateway. These companies do not develop their own technologies. Rather, they purchase motherboards, graphics cards, and microprocessors, which they use to assemble PCs. But these megacompanies are exceptions. As a general rule, you want to see a company spend at least 7 percent of its revenues on R&D.

Spending the right amount on R&D is not the only factor to check. That money must be spent wisely. One way to gauge the effectiveness of R&D efforts is by examining several years historically. Suppose the company spent $5 million five years ago on R&D to build a product. Was the product released within a few years of that expenditure? And how did it compare to similar products from the rest of the industry?

◆ **Revolutionizing a traditional business.** If you're lucky enough to spot a company that's truly changing an industry for the better, you've probably found a winner. FedEx revolutionized a very old business, the delivery of packages, by guaranteeing overnight service. Amazon.com has revolutionized bookselling by bringing its shelves online and building a tremendous Web site.

Look for companies that are able to use technology to find high-growth opportunities in mature businesses; these are usually great investments.

◆ **Creating the standard.** A company that becomes a real industry touchstone can essentially capture a market. Qualcomm, for example, distributed a limited edition of its e-mail program, Eudora, over the Internet. Millions of users downloaded the software and thus made Eudora the standard. Currently, the installed base has more than 18 million users. However, the company did not release Eudora until several years after its IPO in 1991.

But Netscape is a company whose IPO benefited greatly from its standard, the Navigator browser. By allowing users to download the software over the Internet, Netscape quickly became a leader in the Internet. About 90 percent of all Internet users had the Navigator browser by 1995. In August of that year, Netscape had one of the biggest IPOs ever, as the stock soared from $28 to $58 on the first day. It eventually reached $157 (prices adjusted at 1996 stock split).

Another company whose IPO was boosted by creating a standard is RealNetworks Inc. (RNWK). This company developed Real Audio and Video, which allows for audio/video on the Web. The company gave its software away but sold its server software (which makes it possible to create the video). In a few years, the company dominated the

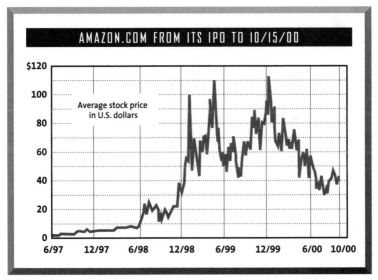

SUCCESSFUL SOFTWARE IPOS

◆ **Quest Software (QSFT).** The company develops sophisticated software solutions for corporations, such as software for monitoring the operations of applications and for managing databases. This was once a sleepy company—that is, until it brought on hard-driving CEO Vince Smith, who was once at Oracle. He took the company public in August 1999 at $14 per share, raising $70 million. The stock ended its first day of trading at $47 and in November 2000 traded at $47.50.

◆ **Agile Software (AGIL).** The company develops software that allows for collaboration between manufacturers and suppliers. At the time of the IPO, the company had licensed its software to more than 300 companies. The company went public in August 1999 at $21 per share. In all, the company raised $63 million. On its first day of trading, the stock surged to $39.88. In November 2000 the stock traded at $75.50.

market with an installed base of more than 18 million. The company went public in November 1997 at $12.50 per share. In November 2000 the price was $26.75.

◆ **Management.** This is a major key in any industry but particularly in a business that is as high growth as technology.

Steve Harmon, who has created venture capital and other investing funds, says, "Overall, I think the most important piece is management. You can pilot the unsinkable ship that brags it cannot be sunk, but how many captains have the humbleness to avert the iceberg? Bill Gates showed he could admit that Microsoft was headed the wrong way in 1995—people often overlook that public admittance. What did Microsoft do? It created an iceberg crusher, Internet Explorer, and put 'antifreeze' in all its applications, including the operating system."[4]

In the remainder of the chapter, we will look at the major segments of the high-tech market that typically create IPOs.

SOFTWARE

SUCCESSFUL SOFTWARE COMPANIES can make you rich. The best-performing technology company ever—Microsoft—is, after all, a software company.

The reason for the tremendous gains is that the software industry has a low cost structure. For the most part, the costs are incurred in paying programmers to write code. Once that is done, the company will duplicate CDs (which costs less than a buck apiece) or sell the product from the Internet (which is virtually free of cost). Then it is a matter of marketing the software.

It is not uncommon to see gross profit margins of 90 percent in the software business. Investors love this—and for good reason.

Here's what to look for when hunting for successful software IPOs:

◆ **Cost cutters.** Look for software products that allow companies to reduce their costs. This is the case with Agile Software and Quest Software (see box at left).

◆ **Flexibility.** Make sure that the software can be tailored to particular needs. Is it easy to install? Is it easy to change? What is the pricing structure? What platforms does the software support?

◆ **Products that travel.** There are many opportunities to sell software to foreign companies. However, the software usually needs to be modified for both the language and the laws and regulations of the nation.

◆ **Ability to withstand the sales cycle.** Complex software may take several months (or even a year) to sell. The reason is that the software is usually expensive and comprehensive. A potential customer wants to make sure he is making the right decision. Unfortunately, such long sales cycles can create volatility in revenues and earnings for many software companies.

◆ **Multimarket potential.** Look for software products that can be used for many different markets.

◆ **Strong focus on marketing.** How much money is the

company spending on marketing its products? Having the best technology is not enough—the products also need to sell well.

TELECOMMUNICATIONS

ALTHOUGH TELECOM MAY SEEM to be at a mature stage in its life cycle, the fact is that only one-third of the world's population has ever used a phone. In other words, the growth potential globally is still huge.

During the past several years, there has been an explosion of voice, data, and video traffic. This has been the result of the spread of such technology as PCs, faxes, Internet access, cell phones, and pagers.

To accommodate this growth, the telecom industry has been replacing copper-based lines, which cannot handle large volumes of data, with high-speed digital fiber-optic lines. However, much of the new technology has been installed within the existing national infrastructure by telecom behemoths such as WorldCom, MCI, Sprint, and AT&T.

Local connections, however, are still primarily the slower, copper-based variety. This has resulted in what's known as the "last mile" problem, or the "bandwidth gap." Top telecom IPOs are the companies that are, in fact, providing solutions for this bandwidth gap. Some of these technologies include digital loop carriers, fiber-to-the-curb, digital subscriber line (xDSL), hybrid fiber coax, and wireless local loop.

Here are some tips for finding successful telecommunications IPOs:

1 Look for companies that can cover their costs. Operating a telecommunications company can be expensive. This is especially the case if the company is constructing a network, as Qwest is doing. When costly projects are in the plans, make sure the company is raising a large amount of money.

2 Favor businesses with telecom specialization. Telecommunications is extremely complex and specialized. This is why it is important for a telecommunications company to

SUCCESSFUL TELECOM IPOS

◆ **Qwest Communications (Q).** Qwest is building a huge network of fiber-optic lines for major telecom companies, businesses, and consumers (the fibers are state-of-the-art lines manufactured by Lucent Technologies). The network stretches approximately 13,000 route miles coast-to-coast. Qwest did its IPO in June 1997 at $22 per share. The stock price in November 2000 was about $46.

◆ **Broadcom (BRCM).** This company develops advanced integrated silicon chips to allow for very fast digital transmissions of data to homes and businesses. The company's technology uses the existing telecom infrastructure. The company offered its IPO in April 1998 at $24 per share. The stock has split and in November 2000 was trading at $160 per share.

have experienced management. The CEO of Qwest, for example, Joseph Nacchio, was the executive VP of the Consumer and Small Business Division at AT&T, where he worked for twenty-seven years.

3 Focus on companies with strong strategic relationships. It is nearly impossible for a company to do everything (even AT&T cannot). Broadcom, for example, has strategic relationships with 3Com, Bay Networks, Cisco Systems, General Instrument, Motorola, and others.

4 Know who the customers are. If a telecommunications company does not have some major customers, then the technology or network may not be good. For example, Broadcom's customers include Ericsson, Adaptec, Cabletron, Digital Equipment, and Nortel.

INFRASTRUCTURE

ALTHOUGH THE INTERNET INFRASTRUCTURE was built for the academic community, in the past few years the Net has exploded with traffic, allowing for e-commerce, sound, and even video. As a result, the Internet infrastructure has had difficulties handling such huge volumes of traffic.

Of course, this has presented immense opportunities for companies to develop technologies that enhance the Internet infrastructure. One example is Akamai Technologies Inc. (AKAM), which translates to "cool" in Hawaiian. The company's flagship product, FreeFlow, helps companies to speed up the transmission of content on their Web sites. This is done by the creation of a worldwide network of servers that use supplicated software to route data in an optimum manner. (There are more than 900 Akamai servers in fifteen countries.) Using the Akamai technologies, some companies have been able to increase the speed of their Web sites by as much as ten times. Customers include such heavyweights as Yahoo!, Infoseek, and the Discovery Channel Online.

Akamai went public in October 1999 at $26 per share. The company raised $234 million. The stock price in November 2000 was around $40.

When analyzing infrastructure companies, it is important to be sure that they meet the following criteria:

◆ **Real time.** Corporate customers want constant monitoring of their networks, measuring their effectiveness. This means getting information in real time.

◆ **Reliability.** Companies are engaging in complex transactions on the Net. They want to make sure that these transactions are completed properly—on a twenty-four-hours-a-day, seven-days-a-week basis.

◆ **Security.** Increasingly, companies are placing sensitive data on the Net. If there is a breach of this data, it could pose serious problems in terms of credibility and liability exposure.

◆ **Exponential improvement.** Implementing new technologies in a corporation is no easy task. It can be both time-consuming and costly. In order for companies to adopt new technologies, there must be a substantial increase in performance over existing technologies.

◆ **Scalability.** Often companies will be hit with spikes in traffic. A technology solution must be able to dynamically scale according to rapid changes in traffic volume.

◆ **Ease of implementation.** Corporations usually have many technological systems. Thus, it is important that new technologies be easy to install in such environments.

◆ **Necessity.** When the PC revolution first took the world by storm, there was an immediate need for an operating system. A small company called Microsoft provided the solutions with DOS. With the development of the Internet, additional needs have presented themselves. For example, electronic commerce requires security measures, and VeriSign (VRSN) filled the need by creating trust services, such as digital certificates and online identification. VeriSign's IPO was in January 1998 and was priced at $14 per share. In November 2000 the stock was trading at $140. Since its IPO, the company has had two 2-for-1 stock splits.

BUSINESS-TO-BUSINESS

DESPITE THE TECHNOLOGICAL REVOLUTION, many businesses (including large ones) still transact with each other using traditional processes, such as paper-based systems. Of course, these systems are costly and time-consuming. For example, according to a study by a research organization called AMR, the cost of a manual procurement transaction is between $75 and $175.

Another possible problem is "maverick buying." This is when employees fail to use existing corporate internal guidelines for procurement and thus may forgo quantity discounts and other advantages.

Interestingly enough, even companies that use online solutions face problems. The traditional system for online business-to-business transactions is called Electronic Data Interchange (EDI). Unfortunately, EDI requires high-end computers and does not have open standards, which makes it difficult to integrate with other internal systems. This situation has led to a new technology industry, known as business-to-business (B2B). B2B helps link companies together to promote transactions online. According to a study by Forrester Research, the B2B market is expected to explode to $1.3 trillion by 2003, which means there will be a huge demand for B2B technology solutions.

One leading B2B company is Ariba (ARBA). The company has developed a full suite of software solutions—known as the Ariba B2B Commerce Platform—that allows companies to manage the buying, selling, and administration of B2B systems. Companies such as U.S. West, Visa, FedEx, and Cisco use Ariba technology. Ariba went public in June 1999 at $23 per share, raising $132 million. The stock price in November 2000 was $125.

The following are key aspects of strong B2B companies that you should look for when evaluating a potential investment:

◆ **Worldwide solutions.** In order for companies to get the full value of B2B commerce, the technology must allow for worldwide applications. This means adjusting for such complex matters as time zones and foreign currencies.

◆ **Significantly reduced costs.** In order to use a B2B solution, companies must realize substantial cost savings, which means effectively streamlining tedious tasks.

◆ **Network effect.** Companies do not want just to reduce costs but also to find new revenue sources. The more members there are for a B2B system, the better the revenue opportunities. This is known as the network effect.

APPLICATION SERVICE PROVIDERS

WITH TECHNOLOGY MOVING so quickly, it is difficult for companies to keep up. Yet with the advent of the Internet, it is now possible for companies to better outsource their technology needs. This model is known as an Application Service Provider (ASP). Basically, an ASP manages complex computer software applications, such as payroll or sales automation, for other companies. For this service, an ASP collects a monthly fee; in a way, it's as if the customers are renting software. With an ASP, a company can lower its technology costs and get customization, as well as have access to the "best-of-breed" applications. In other words, a company can focus on its core competencies.

As for ASPs, these companies basically rent their services

to corporate customers, usually on a monthly basis—and the market is huge. The Gartner Group estimates that the market will grow from $900 million in 1998 to $23 billion by 2003.

One top ASP is NaviSite (NAVI). The company provides sophisticated support services, such as load balancing, storage, and clustering. In fact, the company is majority-owned by CMGI, and there is a minority investment from Microsoft. NaviSite had its IPO in October 1999 at $14 per share. The company raised $77 million. On its first day of trading, the stock hit $34.63. In November 2000 the stock traded for $8.

When analyzing ASP opportunities, look for the following factors:

◆ **Time to market.** Look for those ASPs that can implement their solutions for customers within a short period of time, usually in less than a month.

◆ **Best-of-breed applications.** This is essential. Companies want to use the best applications, which are from vendors such as Broadvision, SAP, Siebel, PeopleSoft, Ariba, and others.

◆ **Integration.** An ASP must have solutions that fit within typical corporate environments. This usually means that an ASP supports a variety of platforms, such as Windows, Unix, and Linux.

◆ **Customer support.** It is imperative that an ASP have a strong customer support team to address questions, problems, and concerns. If it doesn't, an unsatisfied customer may easily cancel a contract.

◆ **Strategic relationships.** Being a successful ASP means getting customers, and one effective way of doing this is teaming up with partners, such as major consulting firms and systems integrators.

WIRELESS

WE LIVE IN AN INCREASINGLY mobile world. According to International Data Corporation, the remote and mobile workforce in the United States (defined as individuals who spend more than 20 percent of their workday away from the office) will grow from 34 million people in 1998 to 47 million by 2003. To deal with this trend, there will be a growing reliance on wireless applications. For example, according to Jupiter Communications, shipments of advanced pagers and electronic personal organizers that can access the Web will grow from 1.8 million in 1998 to 9.4 million by 2002.

An IPO that benefited immensely from wireless was Aether Systems Inc. (AETH). The company is a provider of wireless data services and software for handheld devices. Aether originally focused on the financial services industry but has broadened its product line for other uses, such as health care, logistics, and sales automation. Its customers include Morgan Stanley and Reuters.

Here are factors to consider for successful wireless companies:

◆ **Breadth.** Customers want choice. This means engaging in much licensing of content to make wireless offerings very compelling.

◆ **Standards.** It is important that a company be an integral part of the creation of the standards of the wireless industry. This adds credibility as well as fast-to-market advantages. For example, Phone.com (PHCM) has been instrumental in the development of Wireless Application Protocol (WAP), which is the standard for wireless Internet devices.

◆ **Development.** There needs to be constant innovation within a wireless company. This means having a strong group of engineers. Also, it often makes sense for wireless companies to acquire technology. For example, GoAmerica (GOAM), a top wireless provider, purchased Wynd Communications Corporation, which is a developer of technologies that allow easier communications for the hearing impaired. According to the American Speech and Hearing Association, there are 42 million Americans with varying levels of hearing and/or speech loss who have difficulties with wireless communications.

◆ **Customer base.** A wireless company must find ways to increase its subscriber base. One way this can be done is through strategic alliances.

◆ **Platforms.** It is very helpful if the wireless technologies can be used on different devices, such as the Palm, Handspring, and Windows CE.

CONCLUSION

ALTHOUGH THERE ARE many success stories for high-tech IPOs, they do not provide a guaranteed road to riches. In fact, some of the worst-faring IPOs have been high-tech companies. Examples include Scoop (which went bankrupt), ImproveNet (down 86 percent), VarsityBooks.com (down 86 percent), and Pets.com (the stock collapsed at 25¢ per share). A company may be king one day and dethroned the next. To invest successfully in high-tech IPOs, you need to actually understand the innovation. It requires a lot of work, but the financial rewards may be worth it.

CHAPTER

8

Biotech
IPOs

N FEBRUARY 22, 1997, Ian Wilmut made history. In his lab in Scotland, this embryologist created a clone from a mammary-gland cell of an adult Dorset sheep. The sheep was appropriately named Dolly.

What was once science fiction is now becoming reality. This is especially true in the field of biotechnology. Biotech is a relatively new industry (dating back only to the mid-1970s). Essentially, biotech develops drugs using the DNA code. There might be, for example, a genetic defect that causes a certain allergy; scientists would then endeavor to isolate the defect and to develop a drug to cure the problem.

Although there are many small companies that develop biotech drugs, the major pharmaceutical companies do as well. In fact, the larger companies will typically sign strategic partnerships with biotech firms, because it is often the smaller, focused firms that

Soros strategy on Biotech
Buy on the way up +
sell before Ph announce-
ment

demonstrate the most innovation in developing new drugs. That is, they are not as bogged down by bureaucracy as are the blue-chip pharmaceutical companies.

Some analysts believe that the biotech industry today is where the computer industry was thirty years ago—poised for substantial growth. Currently, there are about 30 commercial products and 700 biotech products in clinical trials.

Of course, there are some major differences between the computer industry and biotechnology. "Their approaches are entirely different from each other," says Nadine Wong, the publisher of the biotech newsletter *BioTech Navigator.* "One is based on machines, the other on humans. Thirty years ago, computers were not available to the public, but look at [them] now: the PC has become as common as a TV and VCR. Products derived from biotech, on the other hand, are not available to everyone."[5]

If biotechnology lives up to expectations, it could revolutionize modern medicine and, in the process, create significant opportunities for investors. Because of the highly technical nature of the industry, it's difficult to pinpoint the companies and products that will be the first to emerge.

Factors fueling the growth in biotech include:

◆ **Revolutionary approaches.** Traditional pharmaceutical companies develop chemical-based drugs. But for the most part, these types of drugs only treat the symptoms; they do not cure the disease. The genetic drugs created by biotechnology companies are designed to prevent the cells of a disease from mutating or to kill the cells that are creating the disease.

◆ **Wider applications.** The biotech industry has the brainpower and scope of research to develop cures for such intractable diseases as cancer, heart disease, AIDS, Alzheimer's, and even manic depression. But there are other applications. Biotech may help create alternatives to fossil fuels or help clean the environment by creating microbes that eat radioactive wastes. There are also attempts at creating computer chips out of DNA structures, an initiative that Motorola has been working to perfect.

◆ **Cost efficiency.** The United States spends $1 trillion each year on health care. Drugs, which are the most cost-efficient means of medical treatment, are allocated 10 percent of that expenditure. And, with emphasis on further cost reductions, drugs are an appealing solution that might receive more focus and increased federal funding in the future.

◆ **Human Genome Project.** In the late 1980s, the U.S. government initiated a program, known as the Human Genome Project, to map the entire human genetic code (a process known as sequencing). Although projected to be complete in 2005, the project was finished in 2000. "It will provide a tool for the biotech and pharmaceutical industry to find or even cure disease," says Wong.[6]

FDA APPROVAL

UNDERSTANDING THE FDA approval process is crucial for investing in biotech companies. Before a company can sell a drug to the public, the FDA must be convinced that it is safe. Thus, if there is no approval, there is no product and zero revenue. It is primarily for this reason that biotech stocks are so volatile.

Here is a simplified version of the steps a biotech company must take to receive FDA approval:

◆ **Preclinical testing.** When a drug is first developed, the company conducts preclinical tests (all tests are governed by the FDA, which, unfortunately, leads to long lead times for approval). The drug may be tested on cells of animals to evaluate its safety. If the drug appears to be effective, the company will file an Investigative New Drug (IND) application with the FDA to get approval to test on humans. Success in preclinical testing does not mean the drug is the next Rogaine or Viagra. In fact, many of the drugs that get preclinical approval from the FDA fail when testing is done on humans.

◆ **Phase I: Testing on humans.** This phase typically involves testing on approximately twenty-five paid volunteers. In some cases, these volunteers are prisoners or terminally ill patients. The tests involve variations in dosage in order to determine the safety and side effects of the drug. Phase I testing can take as little as a month, but it often stretches to a year because of required FDA paperwork.

◆ **Phase II: Wider testing.** This phase is conducted on a much larger group of people, about 100 to 1,000. It takes months to plan and to set up Phase II, which involves determining the efficacy of the drug based on several different doses. This phase determines how much of the drug can be administered and also measures the effect on the illness of various doses. The process can last up to two years.

In many ways, this is the most critical phase of the approval process. About 50 percent of the drugs that have success in Phase II ultimately reach the market.

Biotech-too me hype

◆ **Phase III: The final phase.** Thousands of people are tested in Phase III, which includes placebo-control, "double-blind" tests. That is, one group is given a placebo (which is a sugar pill), and the other is given the drug. "Double-blind" means that neither the patients nor the doctors know who is getting the placebo and who is receiving the real drug. Basically, this test determines whether the drug is better than a placebo. The process can last from two to three years.

If the drug is approved at Phase III, the company then files an FDA application for marketing approval. This can take about one year. After this, the company is free to market and sell the drug to the public.

ANALYZING BIOTECH IPOS

ANALYZING BIOTECH IPOs is extremely difficult for most of us. As you read biotech prospectuses, you will notice some highly technical terms, such as *nucleotides, amino acids, monoclonal antibodies,* and *antisense oligonucleotides.* It's almost as though you need to be an M.D. to understand the terminology. In fact, many Wall Street analysts who follow biotech stocks are M.Ds.

Since most biotech IPOs have drugs that are in the development stage, you are essentially analyzing the stock based on the potential outcome of pending research. So how do you value this research? How can you determine whether the company will pass the final phases of FDA approval? It's almost impossible for potential investors to know how a drug will fare in testing. In addition, when a biotech company's drug fails the FDA approval process, the results for the company can be severe.

For example, in September 2000 Cell Pathways (CLPA) announced that the FDA did not approve its cancer drug, Aptosyn. The stock collapsed from $30 to $9.31 in one day.

On the other hand, if the drug receives approval, the rewards can be enormous. Amgen stands out as the prime example. It was able to produce two blockbuster biotech drugs in 1991, Epogen and Neupogen (each now generates $1 billion per year). The company went public in 1983 at

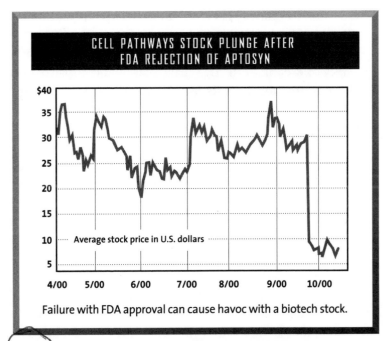

**CELL PATHWAYS STOCK PLUNGE AFTER
FDA REJECTION OF APTOSYN**

Average stock price in U.S. dollars

Failure with FDA approval can cause havoc with a biotech stock.

$1.50 per share (adjusted for splits). In November 2000 the stock was selling for $78 and had a market capitalization of $14 billion. By any standards, this is phenomenal growth.

Both of these drugs were in the preclinical stage of the approval process when Amgen went public. In fact, it was the release of Epogen and Neupogen that initiated a rush of biotech companies going public in the early 1990s— and the value of most of these companies doubled or tripled. Investors wanted to "get in on the next Amgen." So Wall Street placated them.

However, then some of the major biotech companies had problems getting approval for their drugs. Some were running out of cash. Also, there was talk of major health care reform from Washington. The result was that the market capitalization of biotech companies plunged from $49.3 billion in 1991 to $35 billion three years later.

In general, biotech companies go public at an early stage of corporate development, usually three or four years after being founded. But in the early 1990s, many biotech companies were going public too early—within one or two years of founding. This was definitely too soon, and many investors got burned.

Due to the dicey nature of FDA approval and the difficulty of creating effective drugs, biotech company IPOs have historically been extremely volatile. This is a sector that requires exceptional stock-picking skills.

DIVERSITY IN THE BIOTECH INDUSTRY

TO MAKE MONEY IN BIOTECH, you do not necessarily have to invest in drug-development companies. For example, biotech companies spend approximately $60 billion each year on software, equipment, and services to help build biotech drugs.

Here are businesses that benefit from the biotech revolution:

◆ **Information and research.** Biotech laboratories come in two versions: dry and wet. The wet laboratories are traditional; that is, they have test tubes, microscopes, beakers, and other standard equipment. Dry laboratories work with information; scientists take research and try to find a practical way to use it.

Some of the most enticing investment opportunities evolve in the dry laboratories. One such emerging business is known as bioinformatics, which is the process of managing biotech information. Currently, biotech companies have major problems with information overload (for example, there are 3 billion nucleotides in the human genome). Software solutions will allow for the collaboration of scientists; the proper filtering and storage of information in large relational databases; integration of information sources, such as from the Genome Project; and gene simulation and prediction tools. Bioinformatics uses software databases to solve the problem of organizing information and making it available in various formats. The fees for such software can be very expensive, which translates into very high margins for these software companies. One such company, information provider Incyte Genomics, Inc., charges about $5 million each year for its database software.

◆ **Lab chips.** These are microchips that allow researchers to conduct genetic experiments. Besides reducing costs, they also help minimize error rates. A leader in this industry is Caliper Technologies Corp. (CALP). The company went public in December 1999 at $16 per share. In November 2000 the stock was selling for $62.50.

◆ **Biochips.** This technology is also called microarrays. These are sophisticated computer chips that analyze gene structures. With the huge amount of data gathered from the Genome Project, there is a need to organize and make sense of the information.

A leading company in biochips is Affymetrix (AFFX), which went public in June 1996 at $17.375. In November 2000 the stock was selling at $193. The company sells a biochip called the GeneChip, which allows researchers to determine gene expression—that is, see which genes are on, as well as how many. What's more, the technology has the ability to process vast amounts of genetic data.

◆ **Gene therapy.** This is when scientists manipulate a virus by putting genetic material inside it. The altered viruses are then injected into a person to help fight disease. However, gene therapy thus far has had spotty results and side effects. It is hoped that this will change as the science continues to improve.

Collateral Therapeutics (CLTX) is a gene therapy company focusing on such areas as artery bypass surgery and angioplasty. The company had its IPO in July 1998 at $7.25, raising $15 million. In November 2000 the stock was selling for $32.25.

◆ **Proteomics.** With the completion of the Human Genome Project, there is a need to develop innovative techniques to make use of the research. This is what proteomics does. Basically, it is the cataloging and analysis of the 500,000 to 2 million proteins in the human body by their similarities, structure, and patterns. So far, no proteomics companies have gone public.

◆ **Instruments.** To develop drugs, biotech companies need sophisticated equipment. In fact, the development of this equipment has made great strides in speeding up the drug development process. Companies that manufacture such equipment include PerSeptive Biosystems (PBIO), Biacore International (BCORY), and Molecular Dynamics (MDYN).

◆ **Contract research organizations.** These are third-party organizations that help biotech companies recruit patients, design clinical trials, and monitor tests. Parexel (PRXL) and BioReliance (BREL) are both contract research organizations.

STRATEGIES FOR INVESTING IN BIOTECH IPOS

"EVALUATING INITIAL PUBLIC offerings of biotechnology companies, like all IPOs, is subjective," says Wong. "The major problem is the lack of a track record, which makes it difficult to assess the investment and to make a sound decision."[7]

The following is the life cycle of a successful biotech IPO: When the company goes public, the market valuation is typically about $100 million. By the time the company reaches Phase III, it can have a market capitalization of $300 million to $500 million. However, if the company gets approval for its drug, the stock is likely to have a market capitalization of well over $1 billion. The reason for this large increase in value is that a biotech company, when it has a product that is selling, has high margins. Companies such as Amgen and Genzyme have margins close to 80 percent.

Before investing in any biotech IPO, take a look at the company's Web site. You're likely to see a wealth of information on the company, and perhaps you'll even begin to understand the science. Most important, you'll also see what drugs the company has under development and what stages of FDA approval they are in. There is also a Web site detailing FDA clinical trials, called Center Watch (www.centerwatch.com), which has an abundance of useful information. You can also visit the FDA site at www.fda.

gov. These are some factors to look for as you research biotech IPOs:

◆ **Experienced management.** As with any IPO, look for a management team with a track record. It is always reassuring if the management has been able to bring a successful drug to market previously. "A company needs to have a balance of business savvy and technical skills,"[8] says Wong.

◆ **Cash position.** "After an IPO, the company should have lots of cash—at least enough to last two years," according to Wong.[9] It takes at least that long to develop a biotech drug, and the process requires a lot of spending.

◆ **Market potential.** Look for companies that have drugs aimed at major markets. For example, cancer treatment is a huge area (it is the second leading cause of death in the United States). Every year, 1.4 million new cases of cancer are diagnosed, and about 70 percent of all cancer patients receive some form of radiation and 50 percent receive chemotherapy, both of which are painful and fraught with side affects. Thus, there is ample room for new and better treatments.

◆ **Pipeline.** Look for companies with a minimum of two drugs under development, in at least Phase II of the process. If one drug fails to get approval, the company can focus on the other one.

◆ **Strategic partners.** Look for biotech companies with strong ties to major pharmaceutical companies. First of all, alliances provide biotech companies with much-needed capital. Most of these deals involve prepaid royalties on future sales, as well as direct investment. Second, alliances allow biotech companies to take advantage of their partners' resources, such as research, employees, and marketing. Finally, the strategic partnership validates the biotech company. In other words, a major pharmaceutical company believes there is potential in the biotech company's technology and is willing to put money and resources into it.

CURRENT AND FUTURE PROSPECTS

ONE EXAMPLE OF A successful biotech IPO is Maxygen (MAXY). The company is a leader in a new field known as directed molecular evolution. This is a way to modify genes for commercial use. The company's main product, called MolecularBreeding, uses sophisticated techniques to manage the huge amounts of genetic information and develop new genes for specific uses. Potential markets include the chemical, agricultural, and pharmaceutical industries. The company has formed alliances with such top companies as Novo Nordisk, DuPont/Pioneer Hi-Bred, and AstraZeneca.

The company had its IPO in December 1999. The IPO price was $16 per share, and on its first day of trading the stock hit $42.06 (the company raised $96 million). In November 2000 the stock was trading at about $40.

With the aging of the population around the world and the need to find more cost-effective means for health care, biotech companies are in a position for strong future growth.

To find out more about the biotechnology industry, take a look at these resources:

BioTech Navigator
Newsletter written by Scott and Nadine Wong
Sample issue available on the Web at www.biotechnav.com

Medical Technology Stock Letter
Newsletter written by James McCamant
    Piedmont Venture Group
    P.O. Box 40460
    Berkeley, CA 94704
    510-843-1857

Biotechnology-Health Stock Newsletter
Written by Jerry Mullins
    601 Pennsylvania Ave. NW, Suite 700

Washington, DC 20004
202-508-1475

California Technology Stock Letter
Written by Michael Murphy
510-726-8495

CHAPTER

Finance Sector IPOs

DURING THE LATE 1990s, financial stocks soared along with the rising stock market. For example, the venerable investment bank Goldman Sachs Group Inc. (GS) went public in May 1999. The offering price was $53, and the company raised $3.6 billion. In November 2000 the stock was trading at around $90, for a market capitalization of $47 billion.

But the outlook wasn't always this rosy in the financial sector. During the early 1990s the financial industry was looking rather bleak as bad loans for real estate, leveraged buyouts, and credit card delinquencies nearly sank major institutions such as Citicorp and Bank of America.

Today, however, there is close to $18 billion in financial sector mutual funds, providing an ongoing demand for finance company IPOs. The finance sector is quite broad, including banking, mutual funds, brokerages, and insurance sectors. Let's take a look at each area and its IPO performance.

BANKING

BANKING HAS BEEN a very hot sector for several years. The momentum in banking is due in part to favorable economic trends, including the following:

◆ **A healthy economy.** The U.S. economy has sustained a long period of moderate growth without inflation. This has led to lower delinquencies on bank loans.

◆ **Technology.** New innovations—online banking, ATMs, and touch-tone banking—have helped banks cut costs. Automation means more money for the bottom line.

◆ **Consolidation.** The banking sector has undergone a wave of mergers and acquisitions. This massive consolidation has meant lower costs and higher efficiencies throughout the financial sector. For example, bank mergers mean excess branches can be closed, eliminating duplication.

Some of these finance sector mergers have created impressive powerhouses. The combination of Travelers and Citicorp, a deal worth $80 billion, has operations that serve 100 million customers.

Essentially, these institutions want to build themselves into financial supermarkets that serve all areas of the market with a cornucopia of services and product offerings. This will mean more mergers and acquisitions over the next several years. Even with this merger frenzy, there are still 7,000 banks and 1,000 thrifts in the United States.

◆ **Low interest rates.** Financial companies are intermediaries—they obtain money from depositors by paying them interest. They then take this money and lend it to consumers and businesses at a higher percentage of interest. With low interest rates, banks have been able to obtain money from depositors at a very low rate, thus keeping their costs low. In fact, banking is referred to in jest as the 3-6-3 business: bankers pay depositors 3 percent, lend money at 6 percent, and then tee off at 3 P.M.

As long as the U.S. economy continues to thrive, bank IPOs will be a good sector for investors to target. The best bank IPOs tend to be small companies with strong market niches, which is very enticing to major financial institutions that are looking for merger partners. In fact, if the company does merge with a larger institution, the value of IPO shares is likely to increase.

HOWEVER, WITH THE strong gains in banking stocks during the past few years, it's difficult to find bargains, so you need to be very careful. When investigating bank IPOs, focus on characteristics such as these:

◆ **Franchise value.** You want a company that has a dominant position in its market. This is very appealing to big financial institutions that would rather buy an institution instead of building a new market, which is much more costly.

◆ **Fee income.** Financial institutions have been shifting their revenues to fee-based sources—credit cards, mutual funds, insurance, annuities, and asset management. Fee income is desirable because it is less dependent on the pendulum swings in interest rates. A good rule of thumb is to have a financial company with at least 25 percent of its revenues derived from fee-income sources.

Southwest Bancorporation of Texas, Inc., is one example of a successful bank IPO. Regardless of its regional status (it's focused in the Houston area), the company offers products and services that are typically provided by the major banks, such as letters of credit, customized cash management services, brokerage, and mutual funds.

When the company went public, the CEO, Walter E. Johnson, had more than thirty years' experience in the banking industry. From 1972 to 1988, he was president of Allied Bank of Texas, where assets reached $4 billion before it was bought by First Interstate Bancorp.

When Johnson took control of Southwest Bancorp in 1988, the bank had $43.4 million in assets. By the end of 1996, he had built it up to $1 billion in assets. For the nine months leading up to September 30, 1996, the company increased its net income by 32.3 percent, to $7.4 million. The company went public in January 1997, issuing stock at $8.25 (adjusted for a stock split). In November 2000 the price was $37.

Anyone looking at the prospectus would have quickly spotted the positive trends: a pattern of increasing net income, a highly experienced management team, and a diverse financial product line.

DESPITE THESE HEALTHY indicators, there are still many risks involved in banking IPOs. Here are some of the biggest risks:

◆ **Regional problems.** Small banks can be hit hard by a regional recession. This was a setback for the banks in the farm belt during the 1980s and for California banks during the real estate collapse of the early 1990s.

◆ **Liberal lending practices.** If a financial institution has a pattern of making bad loans, the impact can be devastating. When the economy is growing as it has been, financial institutions tend to be more liberal with their lending policies. This kind of leveraging is a danger investors should watch for. *See Buffett q?*

MUTUAL FUNDS

MUTUAL FUNDS ARE one of the hottest growth sectors in the financial industry. Currently, more than $7 trillion is invested in mutual funds.

Much of the growth in this sector can be explained by agreeable demographic trends. The preretirement age group, between the ages of forty-five and sixty-four, will grow from 53.7 million in 1996 to 71.1 million in 2005, according to the U.S. Census Bureau. And between 2000 and 2010 the baby boom generation is expected to inherit approximately $10 trillion from the previous generation. More money means more investing—and mutual funds are a favorite of baby boomers.

According to Investment Company Institute (ICI), which tracks information for the mutual fund industry, at the end of 1997 there were more than 6,800 registered open-end investment companies in the United States. In 1999 there were about 10,000 mutual funds.

What many people don't realize is that most mutual funds are private companies with fewer than 100 investment-professional employees, yet they are extremely profitable. Furthermore, the mutual fund industry is highly fragmented. This usually means there is great potential for consolidation as bigger mutual funds gobble up smaller ones in an effort to increase market share and reduce costs. There has already been a substantial amount of consolidation: Founders Funds was sold off to Mellon Bank for $275 million in December 1997; Michael Price sold Mutual Shares to Franklin Resources for $800 million in November 1996; and the Clipper Fund was sold to United Asset Management for $125 million in May 1997. Marsico

<table>
RECENT MUTUAL FUND IPOS
</table>

◆ **Gabelli Asset Management (GBL).** Yes, this is the fund headed by the famed investor "Super Mario" Gabelli. The fund manages about $23 billion, and there are thirty-two fund portfolios to choose from. In 1999 the fund had sales of $197.4 million and profits of $18.5 million. With 153 employees, the IPO was in February 1999 at $17.50 per share, and the company raised $105 million. The stock was unchanged on its first day of trading, however, in November 2000 the stock price was about $30.

◆ **Neuberger Berman Inc. (NEU).** The legendary investor Roy Neuberger founded the firm in 1939 with a focus on providing advisory services to wealthy individuals and small institutions. Now the firm provides broad-based financial services. In 1999, the firm had revenues of $697.6 million and profits of $135.6 million. There are 1,142 employees and $54 billion in assets under management. The IPO was in October 1999, and in all, the company raised $232 million. The offering price was $32, and on the first day of trading, the stock fell 50¢. In November 2000 the stock traded for $70.

Capital Management was sold for $1.1 billion to Bank of America in June 2000 (Tom Marsico started the fund in September 1997).

Although this sector continues to have more offerings, mutual fund IPOs did not perform particularly well during the late 1990s. It is difficult to find specific explanations. After all, mutual funds have been a fast-growing industry. Perhaps the reason for the bad performance is fear that if a bear market digs in its claws, mutual funds will suffer greatly as investors pull their money out in droves.

Moreover, it is difficult to find an appropriate valuation for mutual fund IPOs since there are not many similar companies to use as a comparison. It is possible that the recent mutual fund IPOs were priced at high valuations. Finally, many of the recent mutual fund IPOs were

offered during a period when the IPO market was showing lackluster performance, which may have put pressure
on the stocks.

Given such performances, it is not easy to find a formula
for spotting solid mutual fund IPOs. However, here are
some commonsense guidelines.

◆ **Invest in the portfolio managers.** Peter Lynch's tremendous success with the Magellan fund catapulted Fidelity
into the stratosphere as it became the biggest mutual fund
company in the world. This is an extreme example, but the
principle holds up. Look for a mutual fund IPO that has
strong portfolio managers with consistently positive long-
term performance records.

◆ **Technology.** Look for mutual funds that are spending
money on information systems that help the portfolio
managers make better decisions.

◆ **Growth.** Look for growth in earnings and assets under
management. The more money a mutual fund manages,
the better, because compensation is based on a percentage
of the assets under management (1 percent to 3 percent).

◆ **Marketing.** A mutual fund needs to spend money on
sales and marketing to increase assets under management.
With thousands of mutual funds competing, sales and marketing are crucial to success.

BROKERAGES

DISCOUNT BROKERAGE FIRMS were introduced in 1975.
Before then, brokerage commissions were fixed. But
when Congress deregulated commission rates, it sowed
the seeds of today's financial revolution. Firms like
Schwab and Quick & Reilly were the first to offer customers low commission rates, which led to much higher
trading volumes.

As a result of these reduced fees and increased accessibility to the financial markets, more people are becoming
comfortable handling their own investments. They do
their own research, set their investment goals, and invest
on their own time. During the past few years, several

online brokerage firms have gone public and have done quite well.

One of the reasons for this success is market consolidation. Many of the major financial institutions have been purchasing brokerage firms at very high valuations. This is likely to continue, as there are fewer and fewer independent brokerage firms. This consolidation helps to cut costs and to boost the industry.

The do-it-yourself investment trend is another significant factor that has contributed to the huge success of the online brokers. There are about 7 million online accounts at the time of this writing. True, this represents a relatively small amount of the total 80 million brokerage accounts. But according to a study by Forrester Research, by the year 2002, there are expected to be 14 million online accounts, with $700 billion in assets.

Brokerage stocks and IPOs include some major risks:

◆ **Market volatility.** A decrease in trading volume would result in reduced transaction revenues and a decrease in profitability for brokerage firms. When times are good, these stocks do very well; in bad times, they suffer. Brokerages are trying to diversify out of the commission business. E*TRADE, for example, offers mortgages and banking on its Web site.

◆ **Price competition.** Increased technology and thickening competition have generated tremendous pressure to decrease prices and, thus, commission rates. For example, E*TRADE cut its commission seven times between 1996 and 2000. So far, increases in trading volume have offset reduced commissions, but this momentum in volume can't continue forever.

◆ **Liability.** Online brokerages are subject to power failures and technological mishaps. This happened to E*TRADE and other online brokerages during October 27 and 28, 1997, resulting in a sticky PR situation. And what if an online brokerage firm is down for, say, a week?

Factors indicating strong IPOs in this sector include:

◆ **Effective marketing.** Schwab, for example, has been in

existence since the mid-1970s and over time has built an incredible brand name by doing smart marketing. Since the online brokerage market is very competitive, upstart companies must gain the attention and trust of investors.

◆ **Reliance on nonprice factors.** To avoid price wars, online brokers are finding value-added services to offer. For example, E*TRADE offers its users mortgages online and has also purchased a company, called ShareData, to provide customers with sophisticated stock option services.

◆ **Distribution agreements.** Online brokerages want customers, customers, and more customers. Because fees are low, achieving a critical mass customer base is necessary for success. Online brokerages have spent millions to get exclusive placements on high-traffic sites like AOL, Yahoo!, or Excite. These arrangements shut out other online brokers, making it more difficult for them to compete. In other words, the newer online brokers will have a much tougher time than the current majors—Ameritrade, E*TRADE, Schwab—that have a large head start.

◆ **Web features.** Another way online brokerages set themselves apart is by offering so-called technological bells and whistles. E*TRADE has an area for online chat, as well as cool Java charting of stocks.

INSURANCE

ONE OF THE KEYS to the success of Warren Buffett was entry into the insurance industry. He saw the great potential of the industry. People paid money on a consistent basis for protection from problems of health, disability, and unexpected death. However, the payment of claims was many years in the future, so Buffett was able to use the large amounts of incoming cash to invest in the bond and stock markets.

The insurance company, in this scenario, is really an investment company. If the portfolio managers are talented and the company does not take excessive risks, the profits can be substantial.

Insurance companies that choose to go public are usually large organizations. It is not uncommon for an insurance company IPO to raise more than $100 million in capital. In March 2000, Sun Life Financial Services (SLC) raised $1.2 billion in its IPO.

When perusing the IPO prospectus of an insurance firm, look for factors that point to the following:

◆ **Brand name.** Look for an insurance company that has *Buffett* strong customer loyalty and brand recognition. For the *franchise* most part, insurance is a commodity business, and one type of life insurance policy is not much different from that of another company. Often, the biggest difference is the price of the policy. To compete in this environment, insurance companies must have a strong brand name in order to attract new customers without having to reduce prices and, thus, margins.

◆ **Reserves.** Look at the risk factors in the prospectus and see if the insurance company has sufficient reserves. Focus on those companies that have a high credit rating (such

---

INSURANCE COMPANY IPOS

◆ **Metropolitan Life Limited (MET).** The company is the second-largest U.S. life insurance company in terms of assets under management. Met Life also provides many other services, such as property and casualty insurance, savings vehicles, and retirement accounts. The IPO was priced in April 2000 at $14.25, raising a staggering $2.8 billion. The stock was up to $15.50 on its first day of trading and in November 2000 was trading at $21.

◆ **John Hancock Financial Services Inc. (JHF).** The company is a diversified insurance carrier, with policies for life, long-term care, and annuities, and also sells a wide variety of mutual funds. John Hancock has about $128 billion in assets under management. The IPO was priced in January 2000 at $17 (the company raised a substantial $1.9 billion). On its first day of trading, the stock hit $17.63. In November 2000 the stock was at $30.

as AAA from Moody's). There have been cases of top-rated insurance companies failing, but such a failure is rare.

◆ **Asset base.** Look for strong growth compared to the industry in terms of assets under management. A large part of an insurance company's compensation is based on how much money it manages.

◆ **Cost cutting.** Look for an efficient organization. Are the administrative costs rising faster than the revenues? If so, such unbalanced spending will hurt profitability and the stock price.

SPECIALIZED ONLINE
FINANCIAL SERVICES

IN THE PAST FEW YEARS, there have been a growing number of online companies that focus on a specialized segment of the financial services industry—such as mortgages, credit cards, or banking. Unfortunately, the IPOs for such companies have been miserable. First of all, there is intense competition, especially from traditional companies that are going online. Also, specialization brings the potential for more volatility if the marketplace contracts. Because of these problems, it is likely that there will not be many more specialized online financial services IPOs. Here are some recent examples:

◆ **Mortgage.com Inc. (MDCM).** On this site, customers can apply and get approval for home mortgages. The company has agreements with fifty lenders, including GE Capital Mortgage, Fleet, and First Union. In 1999, the company had $61.3 million in sales. The IPO was priced in November 1999 at $8 per share, with about $59 million raised. The stock fell to $7.13 on its first day of trading, and in November 2000 was trading at less than $1.

◆ **E-Loan Inc. (EELN).** This company is similar to Mortgage.com; however, E-Loan has been trying to diversify its offerings. For example, the company now offers car loans in addition to mortgages. Although E-Loan has impressive backers, including Charles Schwab and Yahoo!, the stock price has been terrible. The IPO was in June 1999 at $14 per share, raising $56 million. On its first day of trading, the stock shot up to $37. In November 2000 the stock traded at $2.50.

◆ **NextCard Inc. (NXCD).** The company provides Internet-based credit. Customers can easily apply and get approvals for credit cards online. They can even pay their bills online. The company has been expanding, such as into e-commerce by introducing a price-comparison service, and also signing a strategic deal with Amazon.com. In 1999, NextCard had sales of $26.6 million and losses of $77.2 million. The IPO was launched in May 1999 at an offering price of $20 (the company raised $138 million). On its first day of trading, the stock hit $33.50. In November 2000 the stock traded for $9.50.

◆ **Insweb Corp. (INSW).** This is a Web site that operates as an insurance marketplace. More than thirty insurance companies provide their services on the site. The IPO was priced in July 1999 at $17. The company raised about $98 million. On its first day of trading, the stock hit $31.56. In late 2000 the stock traded at $2.

CONCLUSION

THE FINANCIAL INDUSTRY is diverse. Investors should weigh the advantages and disadvantages of each sector and realize that these segments of the industry do not behave exactly alike. However, with the growth of U.S. investments, the prospects for finance company IPOs look bright as long as the stock market doesn't take a major tumble.

CHAPTER

10

Retail Sector IPOs

HD & JJ fall 2019 —
bellwether?

SOME OF THE greatest IPO fortunes have been made from retail companies such Wal-Mart, Home Depot, and Starbucks. The main reason is *scalability*, the ability to sell large quantities in many geographic markets. That is, once you have the blueprint for one store, it is easy to duplicate it across the United States and the world.

But finding the right blueprint can be difficult. The retail industry is rife with competition and reels from the rapid changes in consumer tastes. So to be successful with retail company IPOs, you need to do your homework and have some luck, too. Here are the factors to look for in your analysis:

◆ **Big market.** Sift for retailers that are in markets that have long-term growth potential. An example is the drugstore industry. With an aging population and increased reliance on prescription medication, drugstore IPOs have done very well in recent years.

Stay out of Childrens retail
Ex. Toys-R-US - Too fickle Disney the
exception

♦ **Value/quality.** Wal-Mart founder Sam Walton revolutionized the retailing industry. In his stores, he provided customers with quality products, tremendous selection, and low prices.

A recent retail IPO illustrates this approach well. David's Bridal (DABR) is the largest national retailer of bridal gowns and related wedding apparel. The company operates seventy-seven stores in twenty-nine states and had sales of $175 million in 1999. The retail stores offer a broad selection at great prices. For example, there are 225 core styles of gowns ranging in size from two to twenty-six. So most customers are able to try on, purchase, and take their gowns home the same day. The merchandise also appeals to a variety of income levels—with items ranging from $99 to $899. Prior to its IPO, the company was showing impressive growth rates. Comparable store sales growth was 13.1 percent in 1997 and 18.1 percent in 1998.

The IPO was priced at $13 in May 1999. In early July 2000, May Department Stores (MAY) purchased David's Bridal for $20 per share.

◆ **Fragmented industry with M&A potential.** Look for those retail companies that are in fragmented markets. This makes it easier for an IPO company to grow, since it can purchase smaller retail operations, usually at bargain prices. For example, a key element to the growth of Blockbuster Video was acquiring smaller video chains. Within a decade, Blockbuster Video was the largest video chain in the nation. + OOB 2° Amazon

However, to succeed in a fragmented industry, the management of a company needs experience in mergers and acquisitions. Thus, look for those retail company IPOs that have already successfully merged in the past few years.

◆ **Favorable industry statistics.** A common statistic is "sales per square foot." Basically, this indicates the efficiency of a store. For example, Duane Reade led the drugstore industry with a sales per square foot of $956. This was two times the national average.

Also, look at a company's <u>same-store sales</u> compared to those of competitors. Same-store sales show the growth of stores that have been in existence for at least one year.

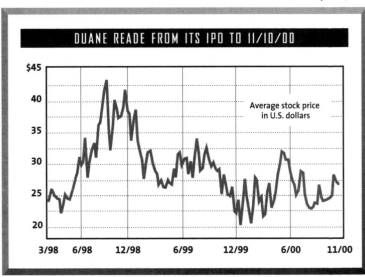

DUANE READE FROM ITS IPO TO 11/10/00

Average stock price in U.S. dollars

Buffett

◆ **Brand recognition.** When you hear the word "McDonald's," you instantly know what to expect: Big Macs, fries. Powerful branding enhances a company's competitive situation. Starbucks, for example, has become the biggest retailer of coffee by establishing an incredible brand name. It managed first to set itself apart and then to stay ahead of the hundreds of other specialty coffee stores that popped up to imitate its success.

BEFORE BUYING A retail company IPO, you should know to look for certain danger signs. Steer clear of companies that have problems such as the following:

◆ **Fad appeal.** Certain retail areas, such as toys and clothing, are apt to fall victim to volatile earnings as a result of fads. When the fad is alive, the sales and profits can be enormous. But, of course, when it ends, sales and profits will collapse. For more information on fads, read Chapter 15.

◆ **Regional concentration.** It is common for retailers to have operations focused in a certain area of the country. The problem here is that if there is a downturn in the local economy, the company can be severely affected. It's better to focus on retailers that have at least some regional diversification. A business such as McDonald's, which has stores all around the globe, is safer because it has many regional markets to rely on.

Many retailers use the capital earned from an IPO to expand their markets. If a company you are looking at has a narrow geographical focus, check the IPO prospectus for diversification plans.

◆ **Weak franchising.** Franchising can be a tremendous way to increase the size of a retail operation. This is what turned McDonald's and Burger King into fast-food powerhouses. But there are risks to the franchising model. Quality is not universally upheld store to store, because it is difficult to control the actions of a franchise's owner. Consistency can be a real problem. For example, many food franchises fail to provide quality ser-

✓ KFC despite a poor product

2018—
20 ?
Dunkin
Donuts

SUCCESSFUL RETAIL IPOS

◆ **Krispy Kreme Doughnuts Inc. (KREM).** The company sells premium doughnuts through its retail outlets (their signature doughnut is the Hot Original Glazed). The first store was established in 1937, and the company now has more than 150 stores nationwide. The company went public in March 2000 at $21 per share, raising $63 million. In November 2000 the stock traded for $72.

◆ **Martha Stewart Living Omnimedia (MSO).** Martha Stewart worked as a model from the age of thirteen. Then she attended Barnard College, earning a degree in European and architectural history. After becoming a stockbroker, she immersed herself in gourmet cooking and then started a catering business in the late 1970s. Her first book, *Entertaining,* became a best-seller, and Martha Stewart became a household name, launching her business empire. In 1999, her company had sales of $763 million. She took the company public on the New York Stock Exchange in October 1999. Priced at $18 per share, the stock raised $129 million. When the stock reached a high of $47.50, Stewart became a billionaire. In late 2000 the stock traded at $23.

◆ **P. F. Chang's China Bistro Inc. (PFCB).** The company operates thirty-six full-service restaurants featuring cuisine from the Canton, Hunan, Mongolia, Shanghai, and Szechwan regions of China. The restaurants feature an energetic, fun, contemporary atmosphere with hand-painted murals and a high level of service. Dishes include Chang's Spicy Chicken, Orange Peel Beef, Peking Ravioli, Chicken in Soothing Lettuce Wrap, Szechwan-Style Long Beans, and Dan Noodles. The company went public in December 1998. The offering price was $12, and the company raised $49 million. In November 2000 the stock price was around $40.

vice and, in general, uphold the standards of a well-run restaurant. And some franchise-based retailers have engaged in accounting shenanigans. Boston Market, for example, was a hot IPO in 1995, rising from $15 to $36. Unfortunately, it accounted for its franchise fees in an inappropriate manner and eventually filed for Chapter 11 bankruptcy protection in October 1998. McDonald's (MCD) purchased Boston Market in December 1999 at a price tag of 15¢ per share.

CONCLUSION

IF THERE'S ONE great piece of advice to follow before investing in a retail IPO, it's this: Visit the retail store. See with your own eyes how business is doing. Is the store clean? Is the service good? How about the prices?

True, this is a subjective approach—but great investors, Peter Lynch included, have made a lot of money using this simple strategy. You can, too.

Chipotle & Dominos) don't care for the food but √6 investments

Restuarants — look for adult staff — not input dey in youngster

11

Foreign IPOs

N O OTHER COUNTRY has as many IPOs each year as the United States. In fact, when foreign companies plan IPOs, they often seek advice from U.S. investment banks.

The U.S. stock market, however, accounts for only one-third of all equity in the world, so someone focusing exclusively on investments in the United States is missing most of the opportunities. The returns in foreign markets can be breathtaking. For example, the Turkish stock market soared an unbelievable 634 percent between January 1989 and July 1990.

International investing can also add diversification to your portfolio, because foreign markets are not always in sync with market cycles in the United States. When the U.S. market is down, a variety of foreign markets will be up. And many nations right now are growing more quickly than the United States is. The stocks in these nations, too, sometimes sell at very low valuations compared to the historically high valuations in America.

Successful IPOs in any market depend upon growth, and foreign markets overall have a lot of room for growth in many emerging market sectors.

TRENDS IN FOREIGN MARKETS

INVESTING IN FOREIGN MARKETS gives an investor the chance to find the next AT&T or McCaw Cellular. For example, there are fewer than 7 phone lines per 100 people in Brazil, compared to 60 per 100 people in the United States. But when the Brazilian telecommunications industry is fully privatized, this situation could change rapidly and present a potentially hot opportunity for investors.

The major phone company in Brazil is Telebras, which was listed on the NYSE Exchange in late 1997. Since then, the stock has soared. Despite this, the stock still sells at a P/E ratio of about 11—relatively low compared to U.S. telecom stocks, such as WorldCom, which can trade at P/E ratios over 50.

Many foreign nations have been and will continue privatizing their main industries. And IPOs are at the very center of this process, because issuing stock to the public facilitates privatization. When a company goes from being a nationalized business to a private one, there is a lot of immediate potential for IPO growth. Here is more about privatization and other developments in foreign nations that create opportunities for investors:

◆ **Privatization.** When a government owns a business, the motives of the company are more political than economic, resulting many times in poor management. But once a company is privatized, it is free to compete and to innovate. Privatization can lead to higher profitability through reduced cost structure, and it provides incentives for managers and employees to have a greater stake in the company's success.

◆ **Proliferation of free markets.** For many years after World War II, many countries were governed by communist regimes. Communism prevented the creation of a fertile market for enterprise as we know it. After the fall of the Berlin Wall, a great many countries moved in the direction of capitalism and democracy. This means that there will be many more IPOs for state-owned businesses. Investors will be able to buy telephone companies, oil companies, water utilities, and other major infrastructure companies that have huge potential.

◆ **Education.** The literacy rates in many countries have been soaring, increasing industry capabilities. Productive workforces are already apparent in such Asian markets as Hong Kong, South Korea, and Singapore, countries with strict educational imperatives. Until the recent slowdown in Asia, these countries experienced tremendous growth. Employees able to maximize innovation and technology create new businesses, unleashing entrepreneurial activity, which speeds growth and translates into increased stock values.

◆ **Technology.** The adoption of PCs, faxes, the Internet, and other modern technology has had a tremendous impact on the growth rates of many foreign nations. Ironically, many foreign countries have the advantage of seeing what has worked in the developed nations. Many emerging foreign countries are using digital and cellular communications instead of analog technologies, because they are more cost effective and offer better quality and features. With a state-of-the-art technology infrastructure, companies grow more easily and more quickly.

◆ **Less protectionism.** Many foreign countries recognize that free trade is vitally important to strong economic growth and have been reducing tariffs, eliminating currency restrictions, and making it easier for foreigners to invest in the stock market. A major example is Argentina, which has undergone radical free-market policies. The result has been tremendous economic growth and strong stock values.

◆ **Demographics.** Many foreign countries are enjoying great improvements in health care, lengthening life spans, and lower infant mortality rates. As a rule, a healthier population means that people have more time to devote to economic activity instead of trying merely to survive.

◆ **Savings.** It is typical for smaller nations to have a high savings rate. The major reason is that there usually is not much for consumers to buy. Additionally, people in poverty tend to be very thrifty.

A high savings rate is fuel for fast economic growth. For example, Singapore has a savings rate that represents 47 percent of gross domestic product (GDP). These savings are invested in new ventures via the IPO market, as well as in existing stocks. With more and more companies investing in these stocks, the values increase.

POPULAR FOREIGN IPOS

◆ **chinadotcom corporation (CHINA).** The company is a lead-ing portal in Asia, with taiwan.com, hongkong.com, and of course, china.com. The company, based in mainland China, has more than 1,600 employees in ten countries. chinadotcom had its IPO in July 1999 at $20 per share, raising $96 million. The stock soared to $46 on its first day of trading. In November 2000 the stock was trading at around $9.

◆ **Satyam Infoway (SIFY).** The company is the largest pri-vate provider of Internet access and services in India. The IPO was held in October 1999. The IPO price was $18 per share, and the company raised $75 million. In the first day of trading, the stock surged to $35.50, and it reached a high of $113. In November 2000 the stock was trading at $7.

◆ **Asiacontent.com (IASIA).** The company takes current Web sites—such as sites from the United States, like MTV.com, CNET, and Sportsline.com—and translates them for Asian markets. Since being founded in May 1999, Asiaconent.com has launched twenty-two Web sites in Japan, South Korea, China, Taiwan, Hong Kong, Singa-pore, Malaysia, and India. The IPO was in April 2000, and shares were priced at $14, with the company raising $70 million. In November 2000 the stock sold for $1.88.

HOW TO INVEST
IN FOREIGN MARKETS

AMERICAN DEPOSITARY RECEIPTS are the best, easiest way for U.S. consumers to invest in foreign markets.

An American Depositary Receipt (ADR) is a foreign company that is actually listed on a U.S. stock exchange, making it much easier to get price quotes—even for IPO shares. Furthermore, ADRs do not require dealing with an overseas broker; rather, a U.S. full-service or discount bro-ker can handle trades.

Technically, ADRs are not really stocks. Here's why:

Suppose you want to buy 100 shares of the "XYZ" ADR. It is listed on the New York Stock Exchange and trades at $10 per share. You call your broker, who phones another broker in Hong Kong, who buys the shares. The foreign broker then deposits these shares in a U.S. bank, and the bank issues a certificate, called an ADR, to your local broker.

When you decide to sell, you call your broker, who calls the Hong Kong broker. That broker sells the shares, and you receive your money.

Even though you receive your money in U.S. dollars, there is currency risk involved in buying ADRs. In fact, the foreign broker is actually exchanging U.S. dollars with foreign currency. This is why there is often a price difference between ADRs and the real stock as it's listed on the foreign exchange.

The other option is to buy directly from a foreign exchange or broker. This preference is definitely for brave souls. You will be paying high commissions. You will need to deal with the headaches of archaic market systems, and you most likely will be required to have a high minimum investment level. Buying direct is more suited for market professionals.

RISKS

IN ADDITION TO OPPORTUNITIES, there are also major risks associated with investing in foreign companies.

◆ **Risk of political strife.** Developing nations are susceptible to wrenching political chaos, which inevitably harms stock prices. Mexico is a prime example: In 1994 there was a violent peasant revolt in Chiapas. Presidential candidate Luis Donaldo Colosio Murrieta, who was to succeed the current president, was assassinated. The discord caused investors to pull their money out of the country, and the stock market collapsed.

But political risk is not limited to riots or assassinations. Perhaps the more common type of political risk is the influence of government policy, such as heavy taxes, a lax monetary policy, or harsh trade restrictions.

However, the most serious threat to investors is when a foreign government "nationalizes" business. When a government takes over a private business, investors lose everything.

◆ **Risk of default.** A default on government debts can have a devastating impact on stock prices. During the 1980s investors pulled money out of third-world-nation stocks when defaults lowered confidence in the economic stability of those countries.

◆ **Currency risk.** Another factor in the fall of Mexico's stock market was the devaluation of the peso. As discussed above, buying foreign stocks involves currency risk, whether you are buying ADRs or buying stock directly. There are financial techniques to reduce the currency risk, called *hedging*. However, hedging is too expensive for individual investors; it's more suitable for institutional investors.

◆ **Market risk.** Every market moves between bull and bear modes—this is normal. However, some countries will attempt to intervene to block market forces. For example, in 1983, when the Israeli stock market collapsed, the government suspended trading for two weeks. Such an action means you have no liquidity. If you need to sell your stock (to buy a car or pay for your education), you are out of luck until the markets reopen. In fact, when a government closes a stock market, investors know there are serious problems, so when the markets reopen it is common for the plunge to continue.

The U.S. market is not immune from having its markets close. This happened in October 1997, when the markets

WARNING

BE CAREFUL: Foreign IPOs purchased by U.S. citizens must be registered with the Securities and Exchange Commission. Click on the "EDGAR Database" button on the SEC's Web site (www.sec.gov) to confirm that the IPO is listed (see page 59).

closed for several hours because of heavy volatility. However, that closure was meant to give investors time to cool off. In that case, it worked out, and the market rebounded.

◆ **Information risk.** It is difficult for individuals to find timely information on foreign economies, because the information may be in another language and obtaining it can be expensive (although the Internet is starting to change this).

The U.S. securities markets have the most thorough laws for disclosure of information. Disclosure requirements in the foreign markets tend to be very lax, almost nonexistent. Different accounting systems and standards, too, can make analysis confusing, and many of these countries do not have many stock analysts. But remember, the lack of information can be a benefit in some cases, because there is a higher chance of inefficiency in the pricing of the stocks, from which a wise investor can profit.

◆ **Custody risk.** Many foreign markets have antiquated payment systems. It can take several weeks to sell your stocks or even receive your certificates. In Russia, for example, stock purchases are registered by hand. Since clears are written on paper (not on computers), it is easy to manipulate trades. In fact, there are examples of companies that have forged stock certificates and bilked investors.

INVESTING TIPS

BEFORE YOU START to invest in foreign markets, it's a good idea first to be comfortable investing in the United States and to build a level of sophistication and understanding of the investment process.

Here are some other tips for investors who are ready to send their money abroad:

◆ **Invest for the long term.** Currency fluctuations can wreak havoc on your foreign investments in the short term. However, over the long term, the volatility tends to be reduced. Also, frequent buying and selling of foreign stocks can be very expensive, since the commissions are high and the liquidity low.

SPECIAL ADVICE ON FOREIGN STOCK

◆ **Try Schwab.** Many discount brokers do not have the resources to provide for investment in foreign stocks. The one exception is Charles Schwab, which has spent a lot of money developing its international trading desk.

◆ **Aftermarket support.** The U.S. market has the most advanced financial distribution centers in the world. In a week, its financial system can handle billions in IPOs; the same is not true in other countries. There is a greater likelihood that foreign IPOs, over time, will fall in price. The reason is that these countries do not have many financial institutions to help support the stocks.

◆ **Research on the Web.** The Web is a global medium and a cost-effective method for researching foreign companies. The best way to get the information you need is to visit a foreign stock exchange's Web site. The Helsinki Stock Exchange page (www.hse.fi) provides access to twenty-two of the seventy-two companies listed (such as Web addresses, e-mail addresses, English press releases, and so on). A variety of emerging-market stock exchanges are listed, such as the one in Chile, which has information on twenty-three ADRs.

Here are some stock exchanges you may want to visit:

ISTANBUL   (www.ise.org)
SANTIAGO   (www.bolsantiago.cl)
TOKYO   (www.tse.or.jp)
SEOUL   (www.kse.or.kr)

You can also find useful information on the Web pages of global investment banks, such as CS First Boston (www.csfirstboston.com) and Morgan Stanley (www.morgan.com).

◆ **Understand cross-border accounting.** Suppose you see that a foreign stock is selling at a P/E ratio of 4. Sounds cheap, right? The stock may actually be expensive, because the country might have different accounting standards from those of the United States. In 1992, when Brilliance China

Automotive Company went public on the New York Stock Exchange, auditors spent 11,000 hours restating the financial data.

◆ **Be wary of economic statistics.** In a myriad of foreign nations, there is a thriving underground economy, also known as the black market. Countries may have stiff laws against certain economic transactions or may not allow charging interest on loans. Despite this, private citizens take their activities underground. In many cases, the government statistics do not account for the activities, which can result in faulty economic assumptions.

◆ **Steer clear of conflicts of interest.** The laws regarding the duties of senior managers and even brokers in some nations can be lax. For example, some countries allow companies to engage in activities that benefit the senior managers at the expense of shareholders—which is often the case with family-controlled companies (these families may even be part of a royal family). Some countries also allow brokers to buy on their account before they make a purchase for their client, known as *front-running*. And, of course, political corruption can have a profound effect on a country's markets. In 1996, Korea's head securities regulator was arrested for taking bribes from companies seeking approval for listing on the country's exchange.

So before you purchase a foreign IPO, you need to do some homework. It often will take you longer to do the research on a foreign IPO than on a U.S. IPO, but it is worth the effort.

CONCLUSION

BECAUSE OF THE DIFFICULTY involved in investing in foreign markets, individual investors should consider mutual funds that specialize in overseas companies instead of picking stocks individually. There are no mutual funds that specialize solely in foreign IPOs, but many funds that specialize in global stocks participate in IPOs and have done quite well in the process.

OTHER IPO
Investments

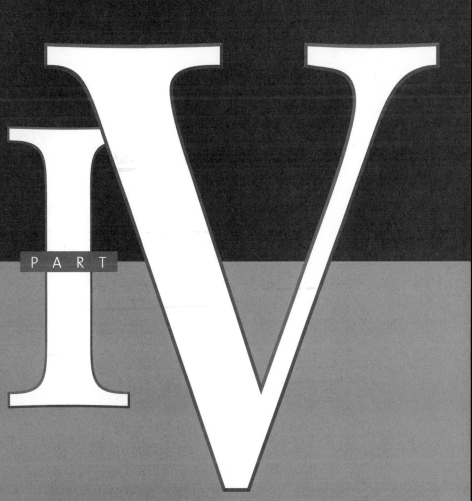

PART IV

CHAPTER

12

IPO Mutual
FUNDS

With more than 10,000 mutual funds on the market, it seems only natural that some would invest heavily in IPOs—and there are several that do. After all, as stated in the Introduction, mutual funds buy a large percentage of all IPO shares. Until now, this has been a well-kept secret.

Mutual funds do not like to announce that they invest in IPOs, because IPOs are risky. But with the recent surge in IPOs, this attitude is changing fast. Renaissance Capital, founded in 1991, is not afraid to advertise an IPO connection. In 1998 it launched the IPO Plus Aftermarket Fund (also called the IPO Fund).

Yes

The fund has been volatile, though. As of the end of July 2000, the fund was up about 75 percent for a twelve-month period. There are about $130 million in assets under management, and top holdings include Genentech (DNA), Sycamore Networks

CK Ren holdings

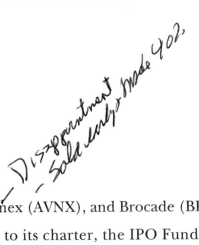

Disappointment made 40%.
- Sold early.

(SCMR), Avanex (AVNX), and Brocade (BRCD).

According to its charter, the IPO Fund has the objective of investing at least 65 percent of its assets in IPOs at the time of the offering and in the aftermarket (which, according to academics, is considered to be up to ten years after the offering). What's more, the portfolio managers are allowed to invest up to 25 percent of the assets in foreign IPOs. Finally, up to 15 percent of the assets can be invested in illiquid investments (these are investments that cannot be sold within seven days).

The IPO Fund does not focus solely on small companies or high-tech IPOs, but portfolio manager Linda R. Killian claims, "Our portfolio is a reflection of what is happening in the IPO market. If a lot of technology companies are going public during any one period, investors can be assured that the IPO Fund will have a high proportion of tech stocks in it."[10]

However, the fund looks for quality deals. As with any mutual fund, its aim is to make money: "We focus only on IPOs that have market capitalizations of more than $50 million," says Killian. "Anything less than that is usually not a quality deal.

"We analyze IPOs according to four criteria: fundamentals, management control issues (e.g., does management own stock?), the trading momentum in similar companies, and the valuation," continues Killian. "We always attend the road shows and often meet with management privately at 'one on ones.' We also dig into the company's relative position in the industry by calling competitors."[11]

A team of portfolio managers runs the fund: Killian focuses on retailers, health care, and telecom; Kathleen Smith covers technology, and her husband, William Smith, researches leveraged buyouts (LBOs) and capital goods companies.

Although there are a variety of mutual funds that invest in IPOs, the IPO Fund is the one with the most focused investment objective.

ADVANTAGES OF IPO MUTUAL FUNDS

THERE ARE MANY REASONS for individual investors to choose IPO mutual funds instead of picking their own IPO stocks:

◆ **Diversification.** For a minimum investment you can get instant diversification. A portfolio manager has the capital to purchase many IPOs at once. Even if one falls in value, it is likely that some of the others will increase in value. This what diversification is all about; it helps reduce volatility. The IPO Fund chooses between twenty and forty companies for its portfolio; other similar funds do the same. To manage this level of diversification yourself would be quite costly.

Diversification is evidently no guarantee, however, since IPO funds typically have wide swings. One example is the H&Q IPO and Emerging Company Fund. After being started on October 29, 1999, the fund gained a stunning

116 percent by March 2000. However, by November 2000 the fund had plunged more than 50 percent.

Something else that may cause volatility in IPO funds is industry concentration. For example, the IPO market may be very hot for wireless stocks, and IPO funds may purchase a large amount of such stocks. If these stocks fall, the funds may suffer greatly.

Finally, an IPO fund may be subject to lockup restrictions (see Chapter 4) on its holdings, which could make it impossible for the fund to sell in a timely manner. It is important to consider such issues.

◆ **Professional management.** Portfolio managers have education and investment experience that individual investors simply do not. They also have a staff to help with the legwork. The IPO Fund, for example, has been doing IPO

NO FREE LUNCH

MUTUAL FUNDS THAT specialize in IPOs tend to have comparatively high fees. Here are some of the different types of fees:

◆ **Loads.** This is a commission to the broker who sells you the fund. Some loads are charged when you buy the fund. For example, if you put $1,000 into a mutual fund and it has a 4 percent load, you will pay $40 in commission. So in order just to break even, your fund will have to increase by 4.16 percent. There are also back-end loads, which are charged when you sell the fund. The longer you hold the fund, the less the commission is.

◆ **12b-1 fee.** This is also known as a *distribution* or *marketing fee*. It is a sales commission that is deducted every year you hold the fund. The maximum that can be charged is 1 percent of your investment.

ugh

◆ **Management fee.** Even if you buy a no-load fund, you still need to pay this fee. It covers research expenses, such as buying subscriptions to investment services and paying salaries for portfolio managers.

research for nine years. Its research database includes proprietary information on 2,000 IPOs. Investors in the fund get the benefit of this research.

◆ **Clout and contacts.** Because of the large amount of money they have under management, the IPO Fund and other mutual funds have the advantage of obtaining hot IPOs at the offering price. Portfolio managers also have contacts, attend conferences, and talk to management. In many cases, they will know about events before they are reported to the public. They may know which IPOs will be hot and which are rumored to collapse.

◆ **Convenience.** You can buy mutual funds over the phone, by mail, and even over the Internet. Investing in IPOs directly is a bit more difficult and time-consuming, so you might also consider calling a broker, insurance company, or bank.

MUTUAL FUND STRATEGIES

HERE ARE SOME tips for investing in mutual funds that have a large exposure to IPOs:

◆ **Use dollar-cost averaging.** Many mutual funds have systematic investment programs: you can have the fund automatically deduct a certain amount, say, $100 or $1,000 or more, from your bank account each month or each quarter. This way, you will not be exposing all of your funds at once but will instead be gradually and steadily investing your money. This strategy is called *dollar-cost averaging*. When the shares are selling at a low price, you will be buying a lot, but when the shares are high, you will be buying fewer. In effect, you are buying low. This is a good strategy for investing in IPOs, since there is a high degree of volatility and the market is difficult to predict.

Reinvesting capital gains and dividends is another great way to use dollar-cost averaging, and most funds allow such reinvestment. But keep in mind: even if you put the capital gains and dividends back into the fund, you are still taxed on them.

◆ **Read the prospectus.** Just as every IPO has a prospectus, so does every mutual fund. Both documents are similar. You'll see information on past performance, the management team, fees, and the fund's objective.

◆ **Ask for help.** Most mutual funds have an 800 number. You should use it whenever you need information on the fund, an explanation of fund performance, or even industry trends. Also, ask how much of the fund's assets are invested in IPOs. Get the most out of those fees.

◆ **Read the proxy statements.** A mutual fund must get shareholder consent to make any major policy changes. This is done via a *proxy,* a document sent to shareholders. Read these documents and vote; it can make a difference. Perhaps the biggest thing to look for is a change in the objective of the fund. For example, suppose you invest in an IPO mutual fund whose objective is to invest 80 percent of its funds in IPOs, and suddenly it wants to lower this to 50 percent. These are things that investors should know. You should also pay close attention to changes in fees.

◆ **Correctly monitor performance.** Compare your fund to others like it. For the most part, IPO funds are microcap funds. It makes sense to weigh your IPO fund against other such microcap funds instead of against the Standard and Poor's 500, which has larger, more established companies and would not provide an accurate comparison.

◆ **Know your fund manager.** You are investing not just in the fund but also in one or more portfolio managers. These people decide what to buy and sell. If a respected, successful portfolio manager leaves the fund, then you may want to leave, too, unless the new manager has an investment philosophy you believe in.

◆ **Know the fund's holdings.** You can request information from the mutual fund that shows the top holdings. What types of companies does the fund own? Are IPOs in the top holdings? If so, are they the type of companies you feel comfortable investing in?

IPO FUNDS

MORE ON THE IPO FUND

THE IPO FUND has a relatively low minimum investment of $2,500. If you want to start an IRA, the minimum is $500, plus a subsequent $100 per month. There are no front- or back-end sales fees, but it does have a 0.25 percent trailing commission per year. The total expenses are 2.5 percent, which is somewhat high for a mutual fund. The fund also has a high (200 percent) turnover rate. That is, the fund will hold onto a particular stock for, on average, only one quarter. In other words, the fund takes a very short-term approach to investing.

"The nature of IPO investing is rapid turnover," says Killian. "When the IPO calendar is strong, we may sell stocks of companies that have achieved our price targets to free up funds for upcoming IPOs. Stocks of IPOs also tend to be volatile, due to the small-capitalization nature of many of them, unseasoned trading, and lack of independent research. So as portfolio managers we have to be responsive to the volatile trading in these stocks and take profits when opportunity presents."[12]

But high turnover can have significant costs. First of all, the fund will incur relatively high transaction costs (i.e., commissions). Second, if the fund sells many of its holdings at a profit, these will be classified as capital gains, which will be passed directly to the shareholders. The reason is that mutual funds are not taxed, the investors are. Therefore, Killian believes that her fund is best suited for non-taxable accounts, such as IRAs, Keoghs, and Roth IRAs.

THE KAUFMAN FUND

THE MANAGERS OF the Kaufman Fund, Lawrence Auriana and Hans Utsch (both of whom have more than thirty years of Wall Street experience), are top-notch money managers. They invest in a variety of industries, such as technology, health care, and retailing, and they look for small market capitalizations, between $50 million and $1 billion.

This duo's investment philosophy is based on scouting for companies with proprietary products targeted at multibillion-dollar industries, class A managements, and strong profit histories of at least 20 percent per year. In fact, before buying a company, Auriana and Utsch interview the management team and its suppliers and customers.

IPOs comprise 30 to 40 percent of the portfolio. The Kaufman Fund has a hefty expense ratio of 1.94 percent. The minimum initial investment is $1,500, or $500 for retirement accounts. Between 1990 and 2000, the fund returned 19.05 percent per year. However, between 1995 and 2000, the fund returned only 12.5 percent per year, underperforming the S&P 500 by 7 percent per year.

MUNDER MICROCAP EQUITY FUND

THIS FUND HAS $34 million under management. More than 50 percent of these assets are invested in IPOs. Munder Microcap focuses on companies with strong earnings potential, superior technology, exceptional management, and market capitalizations below $200 million. The minimum investment is $250, and the expense ratio is 1.5 percent.

The fund has been in existence only since 1997. That year, it returned 71 percent. In the following three years, the fund averaged growth rates of 28.5 percent. In 1999, the return was 57.4 percent, which beat the S&P 500 by 50 percent.

H&Q IPO AND EMERGING COMPANY FUND

THE PORTFOLIO MANAGER of this fund is Ross Sakamoto. He uses sophisticated proprietary analytical models to select his investments as well as to sell them. The models are based on an extensive database from Quote.com, which includes IPO data from 1991 to the present. However, it is important to note that the decision making is not completely done by computers. The portfolio manager provides additional analysis and due diligence beyond the computer models—such as attending road shows and analyzing the prospectuses.

The fund invests a minimum of 65 percent of its assets in companies at the time of an IPO or up to eighteen months afterward. The minimum investment is $5,000 ($2,000 for retirement accounts). In June 2000, the fund had $450 million in assets. After the IPO market plunged in the first part of 2000, the fund started to stage a come-back during the summer. From May through July of 2000, the fund was up 18 percent.

OPPENHEIMER ENTERPRISE

THIS FUND HAS ABOUT $492 million in assets and seeks out undiscovered investment opportunities, particularly in the IPO market. Jay Tracey, the portfolio manager, looks for companies with market capitalizations of $200 million or less. The fund invests about half its assets in IPOs, and the minimum investment is $1,000, with an expense ratio of 1.48 percent.

Check out the Resources section, on page 254, for contact information on the funds listed in this chapter.

13

CHAPTER

Virtual
IPOs

ECHNOLOGY HAS BEEN a driving force in financial markets. It's hard to believe, but Nasdaq, the computerized trading system that handles more than 1 billion shares, did not even exist thirty years ago. There was no computer system that could handle so many transactions. Stocks and bonds had to be traded on a physical trading floor, such as the New York Stock Exchange (NYSE). Now Nasdaq does more trading than the NYSE.

It's also hard to imagine that thirty years ago commissions were nonnegotiable. However, in 1975 Congress passed legislation that allowed brokerages to change their commission structures. The result was discount brokers like Charles Schwab and Quick & Reilly.

Internet brokers have made tremendous inroads in the financial industry. In some cases, commissions are nearly zero. Automation has made low fees possible: there is no need to pay for expensive branches and no need to hire commissioned brokers. Rather, the new-age brokerage firm is mainly an assortment of connected computers, all of which are hooked into advanced telecommunications networks.

ONLINE BROKERS

THE ONLINE DISCOUNT brokerage business's popularity has exploded. Simply put, people like making their own trades—especially at cheap prices. However, cheap prices make it difficult for discount brokers to make money. So these firms are entering new businesses, such as IPOs.

Discount brokers like Schwab, E*TRADE, and DLJ have a huge number of investors and can efficiently allocate IPO shares. Because of this, these firms are able to attract major underwriters.

In fact, these discount brokers stand as real competition to traditional underwriters, and there is likely to be a lowering of such fees. Perhaps this is why several investment banks have teamed up with discount brokers in offering IPOs.

DLJDIRECT

DONALDSON, LUFKIN & JENRETTE (DLJ) was founded in 1959 and now handles 10 percent of all trades on the New York Stock Exchange. The company has more than 7,400 employees and offices around the world—including one in Moscow.

DLJ is a top underwriter of IPOs. It was ranked third by Securities Data Co. DLJ also has a well-regarded research department. Its analysts follow about 1,100 firms. The company was one of the first brokerages to go online. It established PC Financial Network, which is now called DLJdirect, in 1988. This division offers a full range of discount brokerage services, including a variety of online research resources on the site: S&P, Lipper, Reuters, the *New York Times,* Business Wire, TheStreet.com, and Zacks. In fact, DLJdirect even allows individual investors to get access to IPOs at the offering price.

The Resources section, on page 254, lists resources for finding the latest IPOs. Select one that looks interesting, and you can download the preliminary prospectus (it can also be sent to you via mail). There is also an online IPO glossary to help you understand the jargon. If you want to invest, then you can fill out an online Indication of Interest. The DLJdirect Syndicate Department will review your request and determine the allocation of shares.

However, there are two main requirements for participation: first, you must have an account with DLJ worth at least $100,000; and second, on your account form you must indicate that your investment objective is "speculation." DLJ has participated in more than 140 IPOs, including Digex Inc. (DIGX), which manages Web applications for major companies. The Digex offering was on July 1999 at $17 per share, and in November 2000 the stock was selling for about $30.

WIT CAPITAL DISCOUNT BROKERAGE

THE GOAL OF Wit Capital is to provide a one-stop shop for investors, which is why it has a discount brokerage operation. To participate, you need a minimum investment of $1,000. To open a margin account, you need $2,000.

For $14.95, you can trade Nasdaq and OTC stocks (no limit to the size of the transaction) or up to 5,000 shares of an NYSE stock. You can also buy mutual funds (3,800 load and no-load funds from 150 families of funds), stock options, and bonds. Besides making trades online, you can also do so by Touch-Tone telephone or by calling a Wit Capital representative.

You have the option of opening a variety of accounts, including custodian, corporate, investment club, and IRA. You can also make the following types of trades: market, limit, stop, stop limit, good-till-canceled, day, and all-or-none.

Wit Capital has no brokers on commission, so you will not get any high pressure. Instead Wit Capital wants to encourage long-term investing, which is particularly important for successful IPO investing.

WIT CAPITAL:
PIONEER OF VIRTUAL IPOS

IN THE IPO MARKET, there has been resistance to the changes in technology, and there are still many elements of the "old-boy network." However, the Internet is finally forcing change. In fact, online discount brokers are spearheading these innovations. The single most prominent player in online IPOs has been Andrew Klein of Wit Capital.

In 1995, a beer company called Spring Street Brewery, a microbrewery that sells Belgian wheat beers, needed to raise money. Unfortunately, the company was too small to interest a Wall Street underwriter, and venture capitalists wanted to take too much control of the company.

So the founder of the company, Andrew Klein, decided to sell shares of the company directly to investors. One option was to sell directly to his growing base of customers—perhaps by putting a notice of the offering on the beer bottles.

Because Klein had considerable experience in finance (he was once a securities attorney at one of the most prestigious Wall Street firms, Cravath, Swaine & Moore), he decided to take another, more sophisticated, route. He organized the prospectus, made the necessary federal and blue-sky filings, and prepared to sell the offering over the Internet. He posted the prospectus online, and Spring Street raised $1.6 million from 3,500 investors. Overnight he became a celebrity, as the *Wall Street Journal,* the *New York Times,* CNBC, and many other media covered the pioneering IPO.

However, Klein did not stop with the Spring Street Brewery IPO. He recognized the need for a mechanism to buy and sell stock on the open market for companies such as Spring Street that are not on a regular stock exchange. So he created a trading system where buyers and sellers could make their transactions commission free.

The SEC stepped in and suspended trading, but to the surprise of many, within a few weeks, the SEC turned around and gave conditional approval of the online trading system. From there, Klein decided to build an online investment bank, called Wit Capital. It would be a place where individual investors had access to IPOs at the offering price and to venture capital investments. Before that, such services had been provided mostly to high net worth individuals and institutional investors.

Let's take a closer look at the process:

Wit Capital, in association with other underwriters, provides IPOs on a first-come, first-served basis. In other words, there are no special preferences on who gets these shares. You can be a billion-dollar institution or an investor with an account worth $1,000; it does not matter.

To take advantage of this opportunity, you must become a member by registering (for free) personal information on the Web site. You then receive e-mail messages notifying you of the latest new issues. If you are interested in one of these offerings, you can access the preliminary prospectus online.

After researching the investment, you can enter a Conditional Offer to buy a certain amount of stock. These offers are not accepted until the IPO becomes effective, and you can cancel your Conditional Offer at any time before that. Likewise, Wit Capital can revoke your Conditional Offer at any time or reduce the number of shares, perhaps because the firm believes your position is too speculative.

You can enter your Conditional Offer as a *limit order*. This means you can specify that you will buy the stock up to a particular price. This is important, because the offering price of a hot IPO can escalate very quickly.

If there is an amendment to the preliminary prospectus, Wit Capital will promptly send you the revision via e-mail. A written version will not be sent.

Keep in mind that you may not be eligible to buy the stock because of blue-sky or foreign securities laws. If you live in a jurisdiction where the offering has not been registered, you cannot participate. However, in many cases, a Wit Capital offering is registered in all states.

Once you buy the security, you are discouraged from flipping it—that is, selling it for a quick profit. Basically, Wit Capital wants you to hold onto the stock for at least sixty days. This helps promote market stability.

If the rule is violated, you may not get priority for the next offering. Interestingly enough, Wit Capital went public in June 1999, raising $78 million. The IPO price was $9. In January 2000 Wit Capital merged with Soundview Technology Group Inc., a boutique investment banking firm, and changed its name to Wit SoundView Group Inc. (WITC). In November 2000 the stock was selling for $6.50.

Wit SoundView has participated in more than 200 offerings, including the successful Nuance Communications Inc. (NUAN) IPO, which issued shares to the public at $17 each on April 12, 2000. The company is a leading developer of voice-recognition technologies. In late 2000 the stock was trading for $74 per share.

VOSTOCK

IN MAY 2000 Wit SoundView and Investment Technology Group, Inc. (ITG), announced the launch of Vostock.com. This is an online auction site that allows individual investors to participate in the following investments:

◆ **Secondary offerings.** This is the sale of shares that were previously issued.

◆ **Follow-on offerings.** This is the sale of shares of newly issued securities.

◆ **Combination offerings.** This is a sale of both secondary and follow-on offerings.

In the auction, all participants pay the same price (all bids are private). Participation is restricted to individuals and institutions that have brokerage accounts with Wit Capital or ITG. There is a minimum investment of $2,000 and no requirement for being an accredited investor.

Vostock.com is still in the early stage and has yet to have a secondary offering. But when it does, all Wit SoundView account holders will be able to participate. The technology is capable of managing up to 40,000 simultaneous connections with both institutional and individual investors.

The auctions should be exciting—they are expected to last about ninety minutes, and all investors will be able to see, in real time, the bidding action on their computer screens.

PRIVATE PLACEMENTS AND E*OFFERING

IN MAY 2000, Wit SoundView purchased E*Offering, another top online investment bank. As part of the deal, Wit SoundView will become the exclusive provider of IPOs from E*TRADE, which has about 2.6 million customers. In addition to IPOs, E*Offering also allocates private equity deals—companies that have not gone public but are likely to do so or to be bought by another public company. These private equity deals are handled through private placements.

A private placement is a sale of securities that, as the name suggests, does not involve a public offering. Therefore, such sales do not need to be registered with the Securities and Exchange Commission. Private placements make use of a law known as Regulation D, which outlines the details of such a sale, as well as the restrictions involved. The restrictions are strict on who can purchase private placements. One is that you must be an accredited investor—someone who has had an annual income of $200,000 in the past two years ($300,000 if married) and/or a net worth of $1 million.

Traditionally, private placements have been difficult to learn about, especially since there is no public disclosure of the financing behind these deals. But with E*Offering, individuals have a better opportunity to take advantage of these investments. The Web site provides up-to-date information, including private placement memoranda and management presentations straight from the companies that are raising capital. Also, a team of analysts and investment bankers at E*Offering screen each private placement before listing it on the site. They look for factors such as size (companies must raise more than $10 million), proven performance record, large market opportunities, and seasoned management teams. This helps to reduce the risk in these offerings, but it's important to keep in mind that the failure rate for private placements is very high, even if there is professional screening.

To participate in the private placements through E*Offering, you must first submit a form to register as an accredited investor. E*Offering will then call you to confirm your status. According to SEC regulations, you must then wait at least thirty days until you can participate. After that, you will go through the following process:

◆ **Opportunities.** You will get e-mails indicating the latest private placements. You can then visit the site to get the necessary information on the company.

◆ **Participation.** If you like the deal, you can fill out an online form to indicate how many shares you want. You will then receive a phone call from E*Offering to let you know how many shares you will get.

◆ **Invest.** At this point, you send in your check and also fill out and sign a subscription agreement.

HERE ARE SOME OTHER considerations for investing in private placements:

◆ **Holding periods.** Expect to hold on to your investment for at least two years. It takes time for a private company to either go public or be sold. You may also want to check and see if there are any resale restrictions on the stock.

◆ **Illiquid.** The market for private placement securities is very illiquid. If you need to sell your shares, be prepared to sell at a substantial discount.

WR HAMBRECHT + CO

MORE AND MORE, auctions are becoming a popular way for people and companies to do business on the Web. It was the Nobel Prize–winning economist William Vickrey who developed the ingenious auction system. It's the same system that the U.S. Treasury uses to auction Treasury bills, notes, and bonds. Why not use it for IPOs?

Actually, a firm called WR Hambrecht + Co does have an auction system set up for IPOs. It is called, appropriately enough, OpenIPO. The founder of the firm is William R. Hambrecht, who is also the founder of the traditional investment bank Hambrecht & Quist. He started the firm because he wanted to "balance the interests of companies and investors." OpenIPO allocates IPOs to the highest bidders. However, the auction is private, and all winning bidders get the same price.

OPENIPO

HERE'S HOW IT WORKS: Suppose that XYZ wants to go public and has offered to sell 1 million shares. Its investment bankers have performed the necessary due diligence and have established a price range of $10 to $14. Anyone can go to OpenIPO—rich or poor, individuals or institutions—to place a bid on the shares.

Let's say you want to bid for 1,000 shares of XYZ at a

price of $14 a share. Before you can make the bid, you must first establish an online OpenIPO brokerage account for a minimum of $2,000. Keep in mind, though, that when bidding on an IPO you will need to have enough cash to cover the maximum IPO bid price. It is important also to take note of the fee schedule listed on the Web site. What's more, you cannot buy IPO shares on margin, and the minimum bid is for 100 shares, although there is no maximum. You can submit multiple bids, say 2,000 shares at $13 and 1,000 shares at $11, and so on. If you have second thoughts, you can withdraw any of the bids.

Let's say there is a lot of action for the XYZ IPO, and many bids come in (the auctions typically last between three and five weeks before an IPO is declared effective). The OpenIPO proprietary software processes these bids. It determines that at a price of $13 per share, 1.1 million shares will be purchased. This is known as the "clearing price."

Since there are more shares demanded than have been offered for sale, XYZ has two choices. First, it can have the IPO at $13 per share, in which case you will get 91 percent of your bid. (This is calculated as 1 million divided by 1.1 million, or 0.91. As a result, you get 910 shares, which is 91 percent of 1,000.) Or second, XYZ can decide to lower the price below the clearing price. Suppose it lowers the price to $12. At that price, there is demand for 1.3 million shares, which means a 77 percent ratio. Thus, you get 770 shares (77 percent of 1,000).

TRADITIONAL IPOS

WR HAMBRECHT + CO ALSO PROVIDES access to IPOs without using the OpenIPO system. That is, the IPOs are distributed in a way similar to Wit SoundView's method. The allocation is based on factors such as trading history and investment objectives and size (minimum of $25,000).

In all, WRH+Co has participated in thirty-one traditional IPOs. One example is DigitalThink Inc. (DTHK), a leading provider of online education services. The IPO was in February 2000, and the company raised $76 million. The IPO price was $14, and in November 2000 the stock was selling for $32.

PRIVATE EQUITY DEALS

LIKE WIT CAPITAL, WRH+Co also has a system to allow investments in private placements. Investment professionals from WRH+Co perform extensive due diligence before posting the deals on its site. If there is more demand than shares available for a private equity deal, WRH+Co looks at a variety of factors to determine allocation, including the amount of assets in WRH+Co accounts, historical relationships, and whether the investor is a Qualified Purchaser (as defined by the SEC). WRH+Co is always a co-investor in its private equity deals. Remember that according to SEC regulations, private placement deals are restricted to accredited investors.

FBR.COM

FBR.COM IS THE ONLINE brokerage and IPO distribution division of the investment firm Friedman, Billings, Ramsey Group Inc. (NYSE: FBR). Basically, FBR & Co. distributes up to 50 percent of its IPO allocations to FBR.com customers. And if FBR & Co. is the lead underwriter on the IPO, FBR.com will likely get a substantial amount of shares—perhaps several hundred thousand.

FBR.com uses a sophisticated computer system to allocate IPO shares to investors. If there are more shares demanded than offered, allocations will be made at 100 shares for each account. If there are still not enough shares, then FBR.com will distribute the shares randomly.

You can check the latest IPO filings at FBR.com's Offering Marketplace. Here you can learn about IPOs and secondary offerings and even place a conditional offer to buy shares online. To participate in the Offering Marketplace, you need to set up an online brokerage account with FBR.com. The minimum account is $2,000, or $500 for IRAs.

FBR.com has participated in more than forty IPOs. An example is Red Hat (RHAT), which is a leader in software solutions and services for Linux. Linux is a popular operating system for Web sites. The company had its IPO in August 1999 at $7 per share (adjusted for a 2-for-1 split). In late 2000 the stock was selling at about $12.

EPOCH

AS OF THIS WRITING, Epoch has not launched. But when it does, it will likely have a significant impact on the IPO marketplace.

Epoch is a joint venture between Charles Schwab, TD Waterhouse, and Ameritrade to distribute IPOs over the Net (the agreement is exclusive). Combined, these firms have more than 6 million online brokerage accounts and $780 billion in assets. Epoch also has the backing of top VC firms Kleiner Perkins, Trident Capital, and Benchmark Capital. It would not be surprising to see these firms shift their deals over to Epoch.

The goal of the firm is to distribute IPO shares to those investors who have a long-term view, which allows for a more stable stock price. Epoch has a strong management team, with bankers and analysts from Morgan Stanley, Goldman Sachs, and other top investment banking firms. For example, Scott Ryles, the president and CEO, is a nineteen-year veteran of Wall Street. Prior to joining Epoch, he was the global head of Merrill Lynch's Technology Investment Banking Group. Then there is Brad Peterson, chief technology officer, who was the senior vice president at Schwab Technology.

DIRECT PUBLIC OFFERINGS

A VIRTUAL IPO is a company that uses an underwriter whose customers are primarily online. However, people often confuse virtual IPOs with DPOs (direct public offerings). A company using a DPO does not use an underwriter. Instead, the company offers stock directly to the public. In many cases, these investors are customers or friends of the company. The company, in a sense, is leveraging its goodwill to do an IPO and avoiding the costs of hiring an underwriter.

In some cases, a DPO may be sold via the Internet, as Andrew Klein did with his Spring Street Brewery IPO. He set up a Web site and sold stock in the company directly to shareholders, without an underwriter.

Small companies seeking less than $5 million in capital usually pursue DPOs. In fact, if more than $5 million is raised, you need SEC approval. In most cases, companies going the DPO route have had trouble getting financing from venture capitalists or underwriters.

Until 1995, DPOs were quite rare. In most cases, when a company did a DPO it sold its stock only to its established customers, known as an affinity group. Perhaps the best-known DPO was Ben & Jerry's selling its IPO stock at its ice cream stores. The offering was announced on the bowls of ice cream.

But not all companies have such loyal affinity groups. As a result, DPOs were scarce. Then the Internet arrived and offered companies a huge, cost-effective distribution channel to sell stock directly to investors.

In 1998, 1,360 companies filed for DPOs, according to Tom Stewart-Gordon of the *SCOR Report.* Of these filings, 1,428 were able to raise money.[13] However, it is impossible to get an average price of these DPOs, since many of them do not trade on nationally registered exchanges.

Most DPOs are filed as Regulation A or Regulation D offerings, which are exempted from registration with the SEC. But this doesn't mean that the SEC does not pay attention to DPOs. While the SEC wants to help small companies raise capital, the agency's purpose is nonetheless to protect investors.

SOME PROBLEMS WITH DPOS

THE SIMPLICITY OF putting up a Web page makes it enticing for companies to engage in securities fraud. And yes, there have already been numerous cases of DPO fraud.

One such case is Interactive Products and Services, of Santa Cruz, California. The company raised $190,000 over the Internet from 150 investors. Unfortunately for those investors, the company was a complete sham, and the investors lost everything. Netcaller, the company's only product, was a figment of the founder's imagination, based on a rejected patent application. Interactive Products made false statements in its Web prospectus, and the founder spent the money it raised on personal items such as clothing, stereo equipment, and groceries.

Interactive Products' Netcaller was described in its prospectus as "[A] hand-held cordless Internet appliance which enables the user to browse the World Wide Web, send and receive e-mail messages, have real-time communication through the Internet, and two-way voice communications using Internet telephone software."

Interactive Products actually placed extensive Web banner ads, many of which stated "The next Microsoft is offering its stock to the public over the Internet." When you hear such inflated claims for a product that is seemingly too good to be true, stay far away.

The SEC has established a new Web monitoring group, called the Cyber Force, which is composed of volunteers. Essentially, they surf the Web looking at DPO sites, discussion groups, and chat areas to find evidence of fraud, pyramids, and other schemes. Many of the leads that the Cyber Force gets are from the public. You can post a message to this group on the SEC Web site.

There are other concerns with DPOs, including lack of liquidity. There is usually no market for buying and selling shares in a DPO. One company, Real Goods Trading, did a DPO and allowed its investors to trade their stock from its Web site. In such cases, the transaction is then cleared through an escrow agent. But even this approach does not guarantee a good price for your stock. If you check the Web site, you will see very little trading activity. Another approach is to warn investors in the prospectus that the stock is illiquid and will need to be held for the long term. Drew Field, a renowned expert in DPOs (he has successfully raised more than $120 million for companies), believes that a DPO should "be listed on a registered national securities exchange as soon as it meets minimum numerical standards."[14]

It is not common for DPOs to be registered on national exchanges. According to Stewart-Gordon, of the *Scor Report* DPO database, eight were listed on the Nasdaq, and fifty were on the over-the-counter Bulletin Board. "Most of them have taken a serious hit," says Stewart-Gordon, "as one would expect [when] the only people who have heard of a company are the people who want to sell their shares."[15]

Actually, liquidity really should not be a part of DPOs. Says Stewart-Gordon: "You must remember that the intent of Reg A and Rule 504 was never to create mini Big Board companies. Free transferability was granted so that the investor could sell his shares if he suddenly found himself in need. The original idea behind Reg A and Rule 504 was to give the man in the street the same ground-floor opportunities that venture capital companies had—this was in the days when venture capital companies were small and made seed investments. It was always assumed that the investors would hold on for three to seven years and would probably cash out when the company was sold to a larger competitor or did an IPO and became listed on an exchange."[16]

Another chief concern with DPOs is the absence of an underwriter to chaperone the deal. DPOs bypass underwriters. This means that vital tasks such as due diligence, research, and deal structuring, which ordinarily fall to underwriters, are left largely unmonitored and without expert assistance.

However, Field provides advisory services similar to those of an underwriter: pricing of the stock, distribution and marketing, filings with regulatory authorities, "corporate cleanup," changes in corporate structure, business plan development, preparation of the prospectus, and listing of the stock on an exchange.

One of Field's DPOs was the California Financial Holding Company. Founded in the depths of the Great Depression, the company decided to go public in 1983 by selling $6 million in shares to its depositors and borrowers. Field was able to get two national brokerage firms to support trading of the stock. Within two years the shares were trading at $30 (after adjusting for splits). In 1997 the company was acquired at $60 per share. You can see Field's current clients on his Web site: www.dfdpo.com.

According to Field, to find a good DPO, you are required to do your own homework. There is no brokerage firm publishing research reports on the company. "Before investing in a DPO," says Field, "one should feel capable of making this analysis. This means they should stick to companies they know or are able to understand."[17]

CHAPTER

14

Spin-offs

Unc TAX benefits

(+ complexities)

HEN A COMPANY
(called the *parent*) sells all or a part of a subsidiary or
division to the public, creating a new, independent
company, the result is a spin-off. When a company is
spun off, shareholders have stock in two different
companies. Typically spin-offs come from large corporations, such as Viacom, AT&T, or General Motors,
because they have many divisions that can be split off
and distributed to the public in an IPO.

Spin-offs can be very lucrative. An academic study
in the 1993 *Journal of Financial Economics* shows that
spin-offs beat the Standard and Poor's 500 by 10
percent per year in the first three years of indepen-
dence.[18] What's more, a study by Pennsylvania State
University concludes that one out of seven spin-offs is
eventually taken over at a premium to its current
market value.[19]

In a spin-off, the stock price of the subsidiary is

based on the exchange ratio. The exchange ratio is a percentage of the current stock price of the parent company. For example, suppose that XYZ decides to spin off its Z subsidiary. The parent determines that it will issue 0.92 (or 92 percent) shares of Z to existing shareholders. So if the current price of XYZ is $100, you will be issued IPO shares at $92 per share in Z.

TYPES OF SPIN-OFFS

THERE ARE FOUR basic types of spin-offs:

1 Traditional spin-off

2 Spin-off with equity carve-out

3 Split-off

4 Tracking stock ✓

TRADITIONAL SPIN-OFF

THE TRADITIONAL SPIN-OFF occurs when the parent company distributes 100 percent of the subsidiary to existing shareholders on a pro rata basis. Outside shareholders are not given an opportunity to get shares—that is, until the shares trade in aftermarket.

For example, if company XYZ decides to spin off the Z subsidiary, the shareholders of XYZ get, on a pro rata basis, 100 percent of the shares of the Z subsidiary. However, the XYZ shareholders do not have to pay for these Z shares. Why? Because the company is being divided into two pieces. Once this is done, the shareholders of XYZ can sell their Z stock to the general public.

SPIN-OFF WITH EQUITY CARVE-OUT

A SPIN-OFF WITH EQUITY CARVE-OUT is created when the parent distributes a minority position in a subsidiary to the public.

For example, XYZ decides to distribute 20 percent of Z to the public in an IPO. The remaining 80 percent is then distributed to existing shareholders. Why 20 percent? Because if it were more, the transaction would not be tax-free. In fact, to make sure the transaction is tax free, the parent corporation needs to get a tax ruling from the IRS.

A main reason parent companies like doing carve-outs is that it raises cash by offering the IPO to the public. When a company issues 20 percent of Z, the public must pay for the 20 percent, while the remaining 80 percent is owned by the parent corporation.

For example, when Lucent was spun off from AT&T in 1996, about 18 percent of the company was sold to the public, making this spin-off one of the biggest IPOs ever. Because of the size of the transaction, AT&T feared that there would be undue pressure on the price of Lucent. So AT&T did not issue the remaining 82 percent of the shares of Lucent until several months later.

SPLIT-OFF

A SPLIT-OFF HAPPENS when existing shareholders have the option to swap all or a part of their existing shares for new shares in the subsidiary based on an exchange ratio

WHY COMPANIES SPIN OFF

◆ **Enhance shareholder value.** The main reason for spin-offs is to increase total shareholder value. In other words, management is trying to get the stock price as high as possible, which is definitely good news for investors.

◆ **Get new customers.** A prime example is Lucent. When it was part of AT&T, a variety of customers did not want to do business with Lucent because the customers were competitors of AT&T's other divisions. After the spin-off, business soared for Lucent. *Not enuf*

◆ **Unload.** Sometimes parent companies consider a subsidiary to be a nonessential (or even failing) business and want to sell it off to the public, ideally for a good price. This is a particularly popular practice when the IPO market is very strong. <u>The parent company may even transfer debt from its balance sheet to the subsidiary's. Investors beware.</u>

◆ **Meet legal regulations.** A parent company may spin off because it is in violation of the antitrust laws. This was basically the case with AT&T when it spun off its Baby Bell companies.

◆ **Create easier valuation.** After a spin-off, it becomes much easier to value the parent and the subsidiary. In fact, analysts typically upgrade their evaluations of both when there is a spin-off. Example: Sears's 1993 spin-off of Dean Witter-Discover and AllState.

◆ **Remove "rich uncle syndrome."** A subsidiary that is part of a major corporation can sometimes be shielded from the demands of competition. By doing a spin-off, the subsidiary will, ideally, be invigorated by participating in the market.

set by the parent company. In this type of transaction, no money is raised for the parent company (since the company is merely being divided). A <u>split-off is equivalent to a stock buyback</u>. The parent corporation will attempt to make the exchange ratio attractive enough for shareholders to swap stock in the parent corporation for stock in the subsidiary. The result is that there are fewer shares of the parent company left.

TRACKING STOCK *Berkshire H,*

A TRACKING STOCK is very similar to a traditional spin-off. Basically, tracking stocks are a separate class of a company's common stock that is used to track the performance of a certain business unit. They are not considered spin-offs, though, because tracking stocks continue to operate completely within the parent company. Typically, a major company will issue shares in a division to shareholders, and in many cases the parent company will raise money in the process. Take a look at AT&T. In late April 2000, the firm issued a tracking stock on its wireless division, AT&T Wireless (AWE). AT&T Wireless raised a staggering $10.6 billion. Nevertheless, the response to the IPO was tepid—the price rose only from $29.50 to $31.81 on its first day of trading. In late 2000 the stock was trading for $20 per share.

Actually, sub-par performances are common with tracking stocks. After all, a tracking stock conveys absolutely no ownership rights to the shareholders. In fact, tracking stocks are often called "fictional stocks"—if the company goes bust, you have no claim to any assets. There are other potential problems, such as conflicts of interest. In a tracking stock, the board of directors is the same for both the parent and the subsidiary company. So when the board makes decisions it is difficult to determine whether it is favoring the parent or the subsidiary.

However, this is not to imply that all tracking stocks perform poorly. Some have done quite well. Sprint issued a tracking stock on its Sprint PCS (PCS) division in November 1998. The issue price was $10 (adjusting for a 2-for-1 split). In late 2000 the stock was selling for around $26 per share.

RECENT SPIN-OFFS

◆ **Palm Inc. (PALM).** The company is the dominant player in handheld computing devices. Since its inception, the company has sold more than 6 million devices worldwide. Revenues went from $1 million in 1995 to $564 million in 1999. On March 1, 2000, 3Com (COMS) spun off the Palm division, raising $874 million. The offering price was $38. On the first day of trading, shares soared to a high of $165. In November 2000 the shares were $50.

◆ **Agilent Technologies (A).** This was a division of Hewlett-Packard (HWP), although Agilent itself is large, with 43,000 employees in more than 120 companies. Agilent is a leading developer of monitoring technology for biotech, semiconductors, and fiber optics. In 1999, the company had revenues of $8.3 billion. The spin-off occurred in November 1999, and the company raised $2.1 billion. The offering price was $30, and the stock closed its first day of trading at $44. In November 2000 the stock traded at $50.

FINDING GOOD SPIN-OFFS

YOU'LL SEE ANNOUNCEMENTS of company spin-offs printed in major financial publications, such as the *Wall Street Journal* and *Investors Business Daily*. However, information in these articles tends to be very sparse. Thus, you will need to investigate the company's financial data further.

After announcing a spin-off, a company may take six months to a year, or even longer, to make SEC disclosures. It is possible to purchase shares in the parent company before the disclosures, although this is risky, since it is advisable to read the disclosures before investing in a spin-off. So to play this game wisely, you need some patience.

The SEC disclosure document for a spin-off is the Form 10, which has most of the information needed to make an investment. Usually, the Form 10 will go through several amendments. So make sure you have the latest document. The document is like a prospectus, but usually shorter.

You should also get the company's other financial statements, such as the annual and quarterly reports. If a spin-off represents a large percentage of the parent company, there is also a requirement to file a proxy statement, so that shareholders can vote on the transaction.

Such documents can be several hundred pages long, *as expected* but you don't have to read everything. You need to focus only on certain parts, such as the following:

◆ **Major stock ownership.** Make sure that management has a significant stake in the company. Ownership of 10 to 20 percent by management should be enough of an incentive.

◆ **Pro forma financial data.** The Form 10 contains pro forma income statements and balance sheets, listed as though the company were independent. Has the company done well? Are earnings and revenues growing? Is freeing the company from the parent likely to improve these numbers?

◆ **Big name in the new company.** Look to see if a top-notch CEO will head the spin-off. When Marriott decided to spin off its hotel properties into a new entity called Host Marriott, the then-CEO of Marriott, Stephen Bollenbach, decided to become the CEO of the new Host Marriott company. He obviously saw a lot of upside to this new company. What's more, management was motivated with 20 percent ownership of the stock. Within four months of the spin-off, the stock tripled.

◆ **Market.** There is a section in the Form 10 called "Business of the Company." Focus on how much of the market the company has. Do they have major customers? Is their market expanding?

◆ **Rationale.** It's important to read the section of the Form 10 called "Reasons for the Distribution." Knowing why a company is choosing to spin off can provide valuable clues for investors.

CHAPTER

15

Fad
IPOs

ANIAS AND
fads often drive the IPO market. It loves to highlight
the "next big thing." But in the long term, fads eventually fizzle out, leaving loyal investors with huge losses.

A fad is a huge trend that sweeps the nation, if
not the world. As described in Charles MacKay's
classic book, *Extraordinary Popular Delusions and the*
Madness of Crowds, sometimes people stampede to
buy a product that is of questionable value. But a fad
is short term, lasting, at most, several years. The masses
eventually become bored and move on to something new.

This reality does not mean that you should never
invest in fad IPOs. After all, you have the potential to
make a lot of money very quickly. In fact, you can profit
from fad IPOs even after the fad has become quite
prominent.

One fad that made considerable cash for its investors

Peer
Pressure (handwritten annotation in left margin)

✓

was the Home Shopping Network (HSN). The company was founded in 1977 by Lowell Paxson, who sold products on the radio. Then one day he had the bright idea of selling products on television—thus creating a completely new retailing market. The company went public in 1986 at $18 per share. On the first day of trading, the stock soared to $42. Despite this huge increase, there was more to come. By 1987, the stock was up more than 1,500 percent.

Unfortunately, the company had trouble maintaining its inventory and announced earnings that were far below what analysts were predicting. By October 1987, the stock was selling for $5. *Taken over*

Be cautious: the high rate of return on a fad IPO will usually last a year or two. Then the consumer moves on, and the stock plunges. So it is crucial to be very quick when investing in fad IPOs. These are definitely not buy-and-hold investments.

in + out - flip

SPOTTING THE FADS

SOMETIMES A FAD is not a fad at all. For example, when McDonald's went public in 1965, many thought fast food was the craze of the moment and would quickly fizzle. Instead, fast food met a consumer need that has lasted more than thirty years.

A more recent example is Reebok, which originally sold aerobic shoes. The company went public in 1985 and since then has made many investors rich. Even during the IPO, many thought that Reebok's fame was temporary—after all, it had all the signs of a bona fide fad. After the first year of its IPO, the company soared more than 400 percent.

Fads tend to take some time to develop. For example, even though baseball cards have existed since the late 1800s, it took until the 1980s for them to become a full-fledged fad. Or consider wine coolers. These fruity wine drinks were created in the mid-1970s but did not reach fad status until the early 1980s. So the point at which a product transforms from a mere product into a consumer phenomenon is by no means predictable. And perhaps because of the proliferation of mass media, the past few decades have seen more than their share of fads.

FOCUS ON FADS

MANY FADS ENTERED the market with a novel idea but soon encountered their demise due to increased competition or loss of public interest. After reading their stories, you might think twice before investing in a fad IPO. They can be great moneymakers, but if you stay in too long, chances are the stock will depreciate.

E-TAILERS

ALTHOUGH THE OUTCOME is still not certain, it does look as though the e-tailer IPOs of the past few years were a fad. In their IPOs, these companies raised anywhere from $50 million to $100 million or more, money that was used to

+ games — still here

MAJOR FADS OF THE PAST TWENTY YEARS

Cabbage Patch dolls	Rubik's Cubes
Baseball cards	Pet Rocks
Bagels	Wine coolers
Mighty Morphin Power Rangers	CB radios
Pokemon	Beanie Babies

create consumer brands. This meant heavy expenditures on TV, radio, and print advertising. Unfortunately, creating a consumer brand is no easy task. It usually takes many years, as it did for companies such as Procter & Gamble and Gillette.

There have been other problems, too. The competition is fierce, which has put incredible pressure on margins—and margins have traditionally been slim for e-tailers. What's more, we have seen the emergence of online comparison-shopping sites like MySimon.com (owned by CNET), which put further pressure on margins.

As of early 2000, most e-tailers were in dire straits as their cash positions dwindled to distressed levels. Here are two examples:

NB

◆ **Value America (VUSA).** The company started as a comprehensive e-tailer, selling computers, electronics, office furniture, books, and more. It went public in April 1999 and raised $145 million (the offering price was $23). The prospects looked very bright for the company. After all, it had strong backers, such as Microsoft's cofounder Paul Allen and the founder of FedEx, Fredrick Smith. Despite spending large quantities of money, Value America was still losing huge amounts of money. In early 2000, the company had to slash half its workforce, reduce marketing, and narrow its product line. In late 2000 the stock was selling for less than $1.

◆ **eToys (ETYS).** This online e-tailer of children's products, including toys, software, and videos, had its IPO in May 1999. The IPO price was $20, and the stock hit a high of

---

REASONS FOR THE BURST OF THE BAGEL BUBBLE

◆ **Competition.** The barriers to entry are very low. Setting up a bagel shop is relatively inexpensive, and as a result, many people got into the business at once. With so many bagel shops, there was fierce price competition and not enough profits to go around.

◆ **Consumer sentiment.** Consumers started to realize that too many bagels are not necessarily slimming. Demand started to fall off when dieters cut back on their bagel consumption.

◆ **No differentiation.** For the most part, a bagel is a bagel. Does it really matter where you buy one? In other words, it became difficult for bagel shops to differentiate their product and engender customer loyalty.

$86. In all, the company raised $190 million. At its high, eToys had a market value twice that of Toys R Us. However, the stock of eToys began to crumble and in late 2000 reached $1.50 per share.

PLANET HOLLYWOOD

ON THE FACE OF IT, it sounded like a winner: sign up top-tier celebrities, such as Demi Moore, Bruce Willis, and Arnold Schwarzenegger, to help promote a theme restaurant with a cool name, Planet Hollywood. In a short time the company, Planet Hollywood International Inc. (PHWD), was able to create tremendous brand name buzz. It became *the* place to eat as locations opened up in several major cities.

With such fanfare, the IPO performed fantastically. The offering price was $18 per share, and the company raised $200 million. The stock hit a high of $28 in 1996. But in late 2000 the stock was trading at $2 per share. As the plunge in stock price indicates, it takes more than hype and glitz to make a successful restaurant.

+ Hot day Coney Island

BAGEL MANIA

NO DOUBT ABOUT IT, millions of people love to eat bagels. Several years ago, a variety of bagel companies went public. It was a mania. Ultimately, investors lost lots of money. Here are two of the nightmare stories:

◆ **Manhattan Bagel.** This company went public in June 1994, raising about $23 million. In November 1997, the company filed for bankruptcy because it could not pay its creditors. Simply put, the company was losing too much money. The company was sold and is now New World Coffee–Manhattan Bagels Inc. (NWCI). In November 2000 the stock was trading at $1.25.

◆ **Einstein/Noah Bagel Corp. (ENBC).** Merrill Lynch was the underwriter. The company went public in August 1996 at $17 per share. The stock climbed to a high of $36. The company filed for protection under Chapter 11 of the Federal Bankruptcy Code in 1999 and has since closed seventy-four poorly performing stores. In late 2000 the stock price was 7¢ per share.

TOYS

4+

YOU WILL OFTEN FIND FADS in the toy business. The product life cycle for most toys is notoriously short. True, there are notable exceptions, such as Mattel's Barbie doll, which has been the all-time best-selling toy for the past thirty years.

But for the most part, toys are essentially fads. A prime example was Coleco's Cabbage Patch dolls, which every kid seemed to want in the mid-1980s. As the craze died, so did the company.

Another example is Happiness Express. When the company went public in January 1995, the prospectus indicated that 82 percent of its sales derived from Mighty Morphin Power Rangers. These toys were selling like hotcakes, but the company was burning cash at a frightening rate ($10 million in nine months), and inventories were skyrocketing. All this was explained in the prospectus, but investors bought the stock anyway. When the fad ended, so did the stock. In September 1995, the company announced earnings that were below Wall Street expectations. The company eventually filed for bankruptcy.

KNOWING WHEN TO GET OUT OF FAD IPOS

THE REAL KEY TO INVESTING in fad IPOs is knowing when to sell. Again, there is no exact science. Many fad stocks are extremely volatile and subject to periods of profit-taking. But here are some sell signals to watch for:

◆ **Mounting competition.** This is perhaps the best indicator that it's time to sell a fad IPO. Snapple, for example, did extremely well after its IPO, but it didn't take long for the major soft drink companies to enter the market. Several Snapple clones appeared on the scene at a rapid pace, quickly eating away at Snapple's market share.

The baseball card fad fizzled, too, after too many competitors tried to get in on the game. Because of the success of the original Topps baseball cards, many other companies entered the market, such as Classic, Score, Upper Deck, and Action Packed. There was a flood of baseball cards on the market, and as a result, consumers did not know which ones to buy. The market eventually collapsed, as did the stocks.

◆ **Major drop in earnings.** When analysts are shocked by a fad IPO's poor earnings report, a large drop in the stock price is probably not far behind. This is usually a good time to sell, because in many cases the news only gets worse.

◆ **Drop in prices.** If a company announces its plans to drop its prices, this is a major danger sign. It may mean that the company has large amounts of inventory that it cannot sell.

CHAPTER

16

NA

To Private Investor

Stock
Options and
IPOs

THE PROMISE OF stock options is becoming a very common way for companies to attract talent. In fact, options are offered to employees at all levels, not only to senior management. Several secretaries at Netscape, for example, made close to a million dollars from stock options because of that hugely successful IPO.

What's more, options are a great way to motivate the workforce, because employees' interests are aligned with the performance of the company. Furthermore, it costs a company nothing to offer stock options. This is very financially enticing for small companies that do not have large pools of capital reserved for recruitment.

But not everyone agrees that stock options are a good thing. For example, the famed investor Warren Buffett in his Berkshire Hathaway 1997 annual report indicated that he believes stock options can be a big drain on earnings over the long term for a company as the value of the stock gets diluted—because the company must issue more and more shares. Writes Buffett: "When Berkshire acquires an option-issuing company, we promptly substitute a cash compensation plan having an economic value equivalent to that of the previous option plan. The acquiree's true compensation cost is thereby brought out of the closet and charged, as it should be, against earnings."

Despite this, options are becoming a standard of compensation. It is not uncommon, especially in high-tech companies, for 30 to 40 percent of an employee's salary to be stock options. In fact, a CEO may have 75 percent of his or her income based on stock options. John Lauer, the CEO of the mining company Oglebay Norton, has no traditional salary at all, instead receiving all his compensation in stock options.

Even IPO advisers are taking stock options as compensation. For example, Venture Law, a firm that has been involved in a variety of IPOs, requires that it receive stock options for every company it represents.

But stock options are extremely complicated. Interestingly enough, many senior executives have no clue how these options really work. The truth is that stock options are very risky. For example, if your company goes bankrupt or fails to execute an IPO, your options could expire worthless.

Keep in mind that most start-ups fail within the first two years. In a sense, stock options are a type of lottery ticket. If the company takes off, you win big; if not, you lose everything.

In fact, one of the main reasons stock options have been so lucrative is the sustained bull market. But if the stock markets plunge and we enter a bear market, stock options will be far less appealing.

Before you accept any stock options, seek counsel of a good CPA or tax attorney. It will be well worth the fees to structure a deal that makes sense for you. Because of the complexity of stock option plans, it is not uncommon for an employer to offer a deal that looks promising on the surface but is actually quite risky.

THE BASICS OF STOCK OPTIONS

ESSENTIALLY, A STOCK OPTION gives you the right to buy a certain number of shares in a company for a specified price over a period of time (usually ten years). The exercise price is usually the market price of the stock on the date the options were granted.

But most options have a vesting period. That is, you must hold onto them for a period of time until you can exercise them. The vesting typically begins one year after the hire date and is complete after four years.

There are many potential hiccups in the vesting process. For example, suppose you decide to leave the firm, and you have options worth $100,000. If they are not vested, you forfeit this gain. So pay very close attention to the vesting period of your options.

Furthermore, pay attention to what the options contract calls for when the option holder dies. For example, some contracts will terminate the options, whereas others may give the executor sixty days to exercise the options.

TYPES OF STOCK OPTIONS

EMPLOYEES WHO ARE GRANTED stock options in a pre-IPO company have the best odds for big upside. Typically, these shares are disbursed in quantity and at a low exercise price. For example: suppose your company grants you 10,000 shares at a $1 exercise price, and the stock soars to $50 on its IPO; you now have a profit of $490,000. These returns, though rare, can be achieved nearly overnight.

There are three types of stock options: nonquals (nonqualified stock options), ISOs (incentive stock options), and restricted stock options. The difference between these is how each one is taxed.

NONQUALS

SUPPOSE YOUR EMPLOYER grants you 1,000 nonqual stock options with an exercise price of $1. A year later, your company goes public, and the value of the stock is $20. If you exercise your stock options and buy 1,000 shares, you will realize a gain of $19,000. The company will report the $19,000 on your W-2, and it will be treated as ordinary income. You will then report this income on your current year's tax return. Now, suppose you sell the 1,000 shares in the open market for $20. This will be treated as a capital gain.

ISOS

AS LONG AS THE ISO options are set up properly, you will not pay any taxes when you exercise the options. That is, you do not pay taxes until you sell the shares. The increase in value is treated as a capital gain. However, there is one hitch: the gain is considered ordinary income for purposes of computing the alternative minimum tax (AMT), which applies to many high net worth individuals. One strategy to minimize the affect of AMT is to sell a small amount of options each year.

ISOs last for ten years (after which they are worthless); they typically need to be exercised while you are working for the company (or within three months after you leave); you need to hold onto the options for at least two years from the date they were granted and one year after they were exercised (they can be redeemed if you die). If you do not hold onto the stock options for the two years, they become nonquals. Finally, ISOs are not transferable, they cannot have an exercise price below the current value of the company's stock price, and the amount exercised must not be worth more than $100,000 in any given year (if this limit is exceeded, the excess automatically becomes taxable as a nonqual).

Note: An employer may offer a package that includes both ISOs and nonquals.

RESTRICTED STOCK

THIS IS NOT AN OPTION but rather a grant of stock to an employee. When you receive restricted stock, you pay no taxes. But as the name implies, there is a big restriction: you must hold onto the stock for a certain period of time (if not, you forfeit it). Companies prefer restricted stock because it keeps employees with the firm for the long term while their stake matures.

Let's look at an example: Suppose your firm offers you 1,000 shares of restricted stock. The fair market value is $1 per share. You must hold onto the stock for five years. Three years later, the company goes public at $30 per share. Two years after that, the stock is selling for $100. You have a $90,000 profit. Even if you do not sell the stock, you must still pay taxes on this profit as ordinary income, since the five years have expired.

One option to reduce the tax burden is to take an 83(b) election. This allows you to pay taxes on the restricted stock when you receive the grant. Then, after five years, you will owe only capital gains taxes.

Of course, if you forfeit the stock, you can claim a tax loss only to the extent of what you paid for the stock—which in many cases is zero.

OTHER TYPES OF PRE-IPO STOCK COMPENSATION

IF YOU WORK for a private company, you may be eligible to receive stock appreciation rights (SARs). SARs entitle the holder to receive an amount equal to the increase in the fair market value of shares of common stock from the time the SARs are granted until they are exercised. A SAR can be settled in cash, common stock, or a combination of the two.

There are three types of SARs:

1 Tandem SARs. These allow you to receive the gain as either an SAR or a stock option. The exercise of one cancels the other.

2 Freestanding SARs. These are known as *phantom stock*. Here's how it works: Your employer offers you 1,000 shares of phantom stock at $10 per share. This stock is really not stock at all; rather, it moves up or down based on the market value of the company (for private companies, it is usually an appraiser who determines the market value). If the market value is $20, you will receive $10,000 in cash, which will be treated as ordinary income. You will not have to exercise your shares. It is very straightforward.

3 Additive SARs. Unlike a tandem SAR, this type of arrangement includes both an SAR payment and an exercise of an option.

NUTS AND BOLTS OF STOCK OPTIONS

WHEN TO SELL

ACCORDING TO A VARIETY of academic studies, employees tend to exercise their options almost immediately because of the instant profit. But the real value of options derives from looking to the long term. Selling your Microsoft or Oracle options on the day of the IPO would have been a definite mistake.

NEGOTIATION TIPS

NEGOTIATING YOUR STOCK OPTION compensation package can result in a much better deal. Here are some tips on what to request:

◆ Ask that the company reprice your options if the fair market price drops below your option price.

◆ Ask for a shorter vesting period.

◆ Ask that your options not expire worthless should you decide to leave the company. Also make sure that if your options have vested, you can exercise them when you leave. For example, a top executive of IBM sold $1 million in options one month before he left the company. The IBM option contract specified that if an employee left within six months of exercising options, he or she had to forfeit the gains. The case went to litigation.

◆ Ask the company to provide for cashless exercise of your options. If the company offers loans for such a purpose, ask for a low rate of interest.

◆ Ask what other people of similar position are getting as compensation.

◆ Ask that your stock options automatically vest if the company is merged or bought out.

◆ If some of your stock options are based on your performance, make sure the performance standards are clear. For example, one might be: "Achieve 15 percent increase in sales after the first year."

WHEN TO EXERCISE

THERE ARE VARIOUS STRATEGIES for when to exercise your options. For the most part, it depends on the type of options you have:

◆ **ISOs.** Since you do not pay taxes when you exercise these options, it really does not matter when you exercise.

◆ **Nonquals.** Knowing when to exercise is very tricky. Since you must pay taxes when you exercise nonquals, many people defer the exercise as much as possible. But then again, if you exercise nonquals earlier, you will get capital gains treatment on subsequent transactions, which will likely be at a lower rate. You must also consider the fact that you might want to diversify your money into other investments (see "Diversification," below). Also, if you believe your company will not experience much capital appreciation, it may make more sense to exercise early.

◆ **Diversification.** Suppose you have 100,000 stock options when your company goes public, and the stock price reaches $40 per share. You are now worth a cool $4 million. However, suppose the other assets you own total $500,000. It would probably be a good idea to start diversifying your company stock into other assets. After all, even high-flying stocks can hit the skids.

Keep in mind, however, that selling your stock can be perceived negatively by company executives, who may see it as a sign that you lack faith in the firm's prospects. Nevertheless, such concerns should not interfere with good financial planning principles.

CONCLUSION

STOCK OPTIONS PRESENT many complicated decisions. It makes sense to seek out an attorney and a CPA who specialize in stock options. For example, the CPA may have computer software that will run through various simulations, adjusting for taxes, holding periods, growth rates, and your current goals and financial status. An attorney will help you with the terms of the options contract and integrate the contract with your estate plan. Seeking such advice can, over the long run, save you money, time, and anxiety.

Also, keep in mind that you should take a holistic approach to compensation. Often employees focus too much on stock options and forget that there are other important aspects of compensation, such as sign-on bonuses, perks, and vacation time.

CONCLUSION

NITIAL PUBLIC OFFERINGS are investments that truly get the blood pulsing. They are almost always exciting and risky. As with most things that have the potential for a very high upside, uncertainty is an inextricable variable in the overall investment equation. As discussed previously, the words "hype" and "IPO" are often used in the same sentence. It is not uncommon to see an IPO soar 50 percent or more on the first day and then, in some cases, sink back to its beginnings in a matter of days or weeks.

If I could point to two factors that will make the biggest difference to an IPO investor, I would name patience as the most important trait, and research as the single most vital task for successful investing.

Patience, although a virtue, is more a practical matter when investing in IPOs. The first day of an offering is not always the best time to buy an IPO, because the excitement of the offering can lead to wild

Beyond Wed *9x !*

price volatility. And even if you get the opportunity to *in 3dw*
buy an IPO at the offering price, there is no guarantee
that the stock price will rise. Take eChapman.com
(ECMN), which is a portal site for online finance. On
June 6, 2000, the company set its IPO price at $13.
But when the stock hit the market it plunged, and by
the end of the trading day it was at $7.

If you're looking for a long-term investment, it's
possible to spare yourself from the initial roller-
coaster ride by simply waiting a month or so for the
price to settle down. A stark example is Palm
(PALM), which is the leading developer of handheld
computing devices. The IPO was on March 1, 2000,
at $38. When the stock began trading, it soared to
$165 and then closed its first day of trading at $95.
However, in about a month the stock was below $30,
and in late 2000 it traded at $50. The benefits of
waiting for the speculative buying to settle down can

be great for any IPO investment.

However, before you seriously consider buying any IPO, you need to do the research. Much of this book explains "doing the research," but it's important enough to re-emphasize. The best source of information on any IPO is its prospectus. As discussed in Chapter 4 in detail, the prospectus is chock-full of useful information. Here is a recap of the main points to concentrate on:

1 Does the company have a strong underwriter? Be very wary of new or inexperienced underwriters.

2 Is the company engaged in a sustainable business, or is it a mere fad? If you conclude that it is a fad, you should realize that it's not a viable long-term investment. If the company's products or services are, in fact, built around a bona fide trend, the future returns can be considerable.

3 Is there venture capital money backing the company? According to academic studies, VC backing can be very important for the success of an IPO. A VC firm not only provides the needed capital to the company but also brings alliances and helps to create the strategic vision. Also, if you find that top-name VCs firms have invested heavily in the company, you can be confident that they've done extensive research and are satisfied with the company's chances for success.

4 What exchange is the company listed on? Look for companies that are listed on the major exchanges, such as the New York Stock Exchange or Nasdaq. If the IPO is listed on a lesser one, such as Bulletin Board, be wary.

5 What is the main source of your investment research? Although the Web can be a convenient tool for researching IPOs, not all information found there is reliable or unbiased. Stay away from unsolicited e-mail regarding IPOs, and be careful about chat rooms or anonymous brokers. See Chapter 3 and the Resources section of this book to find information sources that are consistently reliable.

6 What does the company plan to do with the money raised from the IPO? If it is using more than 50 percent of the cash to pay off debt, it will not have as much capital to expand its operations.

7 Does the company have lawsuits pending against it? Legal disputes can be particularly onerous to small companies and become a threat to future success.

8 Does management have experience running a public company? Look for an IPO with managers who have successful track records. ~prev~

9 Does the company have a broad product line and <u>a large customer base</u>? If demand dries up for the firm's major product, the company must have other related products to focus on for future sales. Also, if a major customer goes away, are there others there to fill the void?

10 Do you understand the industry the company is part of? A familiarity with industry trends and major players can be a big advantage in forecasting future success. Whenever possible, focus on IPOs that are in sectors you know a lot about or have an interest in.

INVESTING IN IPOS is a relatively new opportunity for individual investors. With time and practice, the analysis and research required will become easier and feel more familiar. Start slowly, and focus on the companies you know the most about. Do the work before you invest; I assure you it will be worth your effort.

VC – Kleiner Perkin
Sequoia
Benchmark Capital

APPENDICES, RESOURCES, NOTES, AND GLOSSARY

APPENDIX A

THE UNDERWRITING PROCESS

AS YOU INVEST IN THE IPO MARKET, you will see three types of underwriters:

1 Majors. These firms have global reach. They can easily do several billion-dollar deals in a month. They have thousands of brokers spread across the world. For the most part, you will not get a "flaky" IPO from a major. Examples of majors include Goldman Sachs, CS First Boston, and Morgan Stanley Dean Witter.

2 Midsize. These firms specialize in a certain industry or region. They have several hundred brokers. It is possible to find some very good prospects with midsized firms, because they often have special knowledge about a local firm.

3 Small. Be wary of the very small, unknown firms. Simply put, an IPO requires numerous resources for which small firms tend to be inadequately equipped. In fact, the era of the small firm is quickly closing.

UNDERWRITING OPTIONS

THERE ARE TWO MAIN TYPES of underwritings:

1 Firm commitment. CDNow sold 4.1 million shares to the lead underwriters for $14.88 each, raising $61 million. CDNow's officers and directors maintained 67.2 percent of the outstanding common stock. The underwriters, in turn, sold the 4.1 million shares to the public for $16 each. The $4.6 million difference is the profit for the lead underwriters, which is then shared with the group of syndicate underwriters.

It is common for underwriters to get warrants as compensation for services, too. A warrant is the right to buy stock at a certain price—which is usually at a premium to the offering price, such as 20 percent—for a specific period of time (one to five years). The warrants may account for 10 percent of the offering. For example, if the IPO has an offering price of $10 with a 20 percent premium, the underwriter gets warrants to buy 1 million shares at $12.

A firm-commitment offering will also usually have an overallotment option (also called a *green shoe*). This means that if there is tremendous demand for the IPO, the underwriter can issue additional shares—say, 10 to 15 percent of the total stock issued. In the case of CDNow, the lead underwriters had an overallotment of 615,000 shares.

A firm-commitment offering is risky for the underwriter. If it has problems selling the issue, the firm will be left holding large amounts of stock that no one wants.

2 Best efforts. As the name implies, best efforts means the underwriter will try to sell the offering, but there is no guarantee.

You will see best-efforts offerings for small companies that have difficulty raising money. Be very careful if you are considering a best-efforts offering. After all, it should be troubling if an underwriter does not have enough faith in a company to do a firm-commitment offering. Actually, the majors and midsize firms do not engage in such best-efforts offerings. Only the small firms do.

SELF-UNDERWRITINGS

A COMPANY MAY DECIDE to forgo the services of an underwriter. This has been happening with greater regularity as more companies are going public at earlier stages in their business cycle.

Unfortunately, there have been very few successful self-underwritten offerings. As the old saying goes: "Stock is sold, not bought." It takes a lot of effort to get an investor to buy stock in a company. So the distribution channels of an underwriter can be extremely valuable, despite the fact the firm will garner large amounts of fees.

Investors should be very careful of any company that does its own underwriting.

APPENDIX B

ANALYZING THE FINANCIAL STATEMENT ITEMS

THE FINANCIAL STATEMENTS contained in the final section of the prospectus are full of numbers. By using the Ratio Analysis calculations described below, you can make sense of these numbers.

LIQUIDITY RATIOS

LIQUIDITY RATIOS SHOW the ability of a company to pay its debts. The most common liquidity ratio is the *current ratio,* which is calculated as follows:

Current Ratio = Current Assets / Current Liabilities

As a general rule, you want a company that has a current ratio of 2 or higher. There may be exceptions, which makes it important to look at the current ratios of other companies in the industry.

The next liquidity ratio is the *acid-test ratio.* This uses essentially the same formula as the current ratio, except that inventories and prepaid expenses are excluded from the math. The reason for deleting them is that these types of assets are often difficult to convert into cash.

The target number for the acid-test ratio is 1.1.

ACTIVITY RATIOS

ACTIVITY RATIOS INDICATE the efficiency of a company to convert current assets into cash. There are three types of activity ratios:

1 Inventory turnover ratio. This ratio shows the relationship between the amount of goods sold and inventory. This ratio is very industry specific. For the most part, a very high inventory turnover ratio may mean that the company does not have enough product in stock. On the other hand, a very low ratio might mean that the company is not selling its products. In general, the higher the ratio the better, since a company is getting cash quicker.

The ratio is calculated as follows:

Inventory Turnover = Cost of Goods Sold / Average Inventory

To compute the average inventory, make the following calculation:

(Beginning-of-period inventory + end-of-period inventory) / 2

2 Accounts receivable ratio. This indicates how fast a company is collecting payments from customers who are on credit. The calculation is as follows:

A.R. Ratio = Net Sales / Average Net Accounts Receivable

Strictly speaking, you should use net credit sales for the numerator. But most financial statements do not provide that number. Instead, you must use net sales.

As for the average net accounts receivable, this is calculated as follows:

(Beginning Balance of Accounts Receivable + Ending Balance) / 2

The accounts receivable ratio shows how many times the accounts receivable have been turned into cash in one year. As a rule, the higher the ratio the better, since a company gets cash quicker.

3 Days' sales ratio. This shows how efficient a company is with its receivables. The calculation is:

D.S. Ratio = Ending Accounts Receivable / Average Daily Sales

To calculate average daily sales, do the following:

Net Sales / 365

PROFITABILITY RATIOS

AS THE NAME IMPLIES, profitability ratios analyze the profits of a company. The two main ratios are:

1 Return on assets. This shows the operating efficiency of a company; that is, how well the company uses its total assets. The ratio is calculated as follows:

ROA = (Income before interest, taxes, and other income) / Average Total Assets

2 Return on equity. This is a big factor for any investor. You want to make sure that management is getting the best returns possible from the equity invested in the company. The return on equity is calculated as follows:

ROE = Net Income / Average Common Stockholder's Equity

Average Common Stockholder's Equity is as follows:

(Beginning Common Equity + Ending Balance) / 2

PRICE-EARNINGS RATIO

THE PRICE-EARNINGS RATIO is computed by taking the current price of the stock and dividing it by the EPS. For example, if XYZ is selling for $30 per share, it will have a P/E ratio of 30 ($30 per share times $1 EPS). This is a technique commonly used by Wall Street analysts to measure relative valuations of companies. For example, suppose other companies in XYZ's industry sell for, on average, 40 P/Es. Thus, XYZ is selling at a discount of 20 percent of the industry. This may mean the company is undervalued.

However, in many cases, IPOs do not have any earnings (these will come several years later), so doing P/E ratios does not make sense.

Perhaps a better way to value the company is by the price-to-sales ratio. Let's say XYZ has sales of $10 million and a market capitalization of $30 million. Market capitalization is derived by multiplying the current stock price by the number of shares outstanding ($30 X 1 million shares outstanding). To get the price-to-sales ratio, we divide the market capitalization by the annual sales. In this case, the price-to-sales ratio is 3-to-1 ($30 million market capitalization divided by $10 million in sales). This means the company stock is selling at 3 times sales. Compare this to other companies in the industry to see whether XYZ is undervalued, overvalued, or fairly valued.

DEBT RATIO

IN ITSELF, DEBT is not bad. In fact, if a company has low amounts of debt, this may indicate that the company is too conservative. Then again, high levels of debt can be very dangerous, especially if the company hits hard times and is unable to pay the interest and principal payments. The result can be bankruptcy.

The most common indicator of debt levels is the debt-to-equity ratio. It is calculated as follows:

Debt-to-Equity Ratio = Total Long-term Liabilities /
                        Total Stockholders' Equity

RESOURCES

IN-DEPTH IPO INFORMATION

WEB SITES, ONLINE RESOURCES, AND PRINT PUBLICATIONS

Alert-IPO. This is one of the cheapest IPO subscription services available. For $34.95 per year you receive weekly summaries via e-mail that detail which companies have filed for IPOs during the past week. Every day you will receive reports on each company that has filed within the past 24 to 48 hours (www.ostman.com/alert-ipo).

Bloomberg's IPO Center. Bloomberg's Web site offers up-to-the-minute IPO information, including the latest listings, pricing, and links to news stories on the companies issuing the offerings. The site also includes the Bloomberg IPO Index, which measures the performance of IPO stocks during their first year (www.bloomberg.com).

CBS Marketwatch. Data Broadcasting Corporation (DBC) is a leading provider of real-time financial information and commentary. One pertinent section is the IPOnder column, which I write daily (www.cbs.marketwatch.com).

Gaskins IPO Desktop. While many sites provide statistical information on IPOs, few have ratings. Francis Gaskins, an IPO expert, provides ratings on the hot and not-so-hot upcoming Internet and tech IPOs (www.gaskinsco.com).

Internet Stock Report. This is the world's most-followed Internet stock barometer, where Wall Street meets the Web, featuring ISDEX, the Internet Stock Index. Its readership includes Microsoft's Bill Gates, Netscape's Marc Andreessen, and Yahoo!'s Jerry Yang, among others.

I write a free daily online column for the site called IPO Tracker, which frequently covers the latest high-profile IPOs (www.internetstockreport.com).

IPO.com. This site is a comprehensive source for IPO information. For free, you can access the site's database of prior and upcoming IPOs. What's more, the site has expanded coverage of private equity financing, such as venture capital. There are also great charts, including the best- and worst-performing IPOs. You can access useful calendars of upcoming IPOs, as well as quiet-period and lockup-period expirations. The site also has interesting articles about IPOs and investment strategies (www.ipo.com).

IPO Central. This is one of the best IPO sites on the Web. It is a joint venture between Hoover's and EDGAR Online (www.ipocentral.com).

IPO Intelligence Online. Renaissance Capital Corporation of Greenwich, Connecticut, has been providing research to institutional investors since 1992. It runs the IPO Plus Aftermarket Fund. The site carries knowledgeable research and averages 2 to 3 million Web site hits a month. Free IPO coverage includes breaking news; filings; calendars, including companies expected to go public; profiles that eliminate questionable or tiny IPOs; commentary; a complete glossary; a guide to help individual investors; chat; "IPO of the Week"; and lists of Best, Worst, Foreign, and Largest IPOs. Full, six-page institutional research reports can be ordered for $50 each. The site also covers open-end mutual funds, the IPO Plus Aftermarket Fund (IPOSX), NAV information, top holdings, and fund news. Prospective investors can download the fund prospectus and applications (www.ipo-fund.com).

IPOLockup.com. As discussed earlier in this book, an effective strategy is to buy IPOs when their lockup period expires. A stock's price often will fall once employees, officers, directors, and major investors are allowed to sell their shares. As for IPOLockup.com, the site provides updates of upcoming lockup expirations. It first began tracking lockup expirations on October 1, 1999 (www.ipolockup.com).

IPO Maven. The IPO Maven site is managed by Manish Shah, a widely quoted authority on the IPO market (www.ipomaven.com).

IPO Monitor. IPO Monitor provides a comprehensive set of services for IPO information. The subscription fee is $29 per month or $290 per year (www.ipomonitor.com).

IPOPros.com. TheStreet.com bought this company, which provides exclusive coverage of the IPO market. You have access to the latest IPO news, as well as commentary. Further, the site provides recommendations for upcoming IPOs. A one-year subscription costs $255 (www.ipopros.com).

Red Herring. The *Red Herring* is both a magazine and an online publication. The Web site has an IPO news section as well as a free IPO Critic e-newsletter. It covers the high-tech sector. It's a great resource for information about the hottest IPOs and for interviews with the movers and shakers. Plus, there's great industry analysis. A one-year subscription to the print edition is $49 (800-627-4931; www.redherring.com).

> *Red Herring*
> P.O. Box 54560
> Boulder, CO 80322

Upside Magazine. Again, both a magazine and an online publication focusing on high-tech companies (888-998-7743; www.upside.com).

> *Upside*
> P.O. Box 3259
> Northbrook, IL 60065

EDGAR RESOURCES

EDGAR. The SEC manages the Electronic Data Gathering Analysis and Retrieval database of financial filings. You can't afford to invest in IPOs without using the SEC's EDGAR data or frequenting another site that uses EDGAR's information (www.sec.gov).

Other very useful EDGAR sites are:

EDGAR Online. EDGAR Online provides real-time access to financial filings from the SEC. There is a subscription cost but also many benefits. The subscriptions start at $9.95 per month; the fee is based on how many filings you download. There are also free services (www.edgar-online.com).

FreeEDGAR. So far, FreeEDGAR is the only company offering free, unlimited access to real-time corporate data filed with the Securities and Exchange Commission (www. freeedgar.com).

IPO NEWSLETTERS

◆ *The IPO Reporter.* Editor, Omar Sacirbey (212-765-5311).
> 1290 Sixth Avenue, 36th Floor
> New York, NY 10104

◆ *The IPO Trader.* An annual subscription costs $199 (800-436-1295).
> Marketing & Publishing Associates
> 702 Cathedral Street
> Baltimore, MD 20201

MUTUAL FUNDS THAT INVEST IN IPOS

◆ **The Internet Fund, Inc.** Portfolio manager, Ryan Jacob (888-FUND-WWW; www.theinternetfund.com).
> 344 Van Buren Street
> North Babylon, NY 11704-3013

◆ **Kaufman Fund.** Managers, Lawrence Auriana and Hans Utsch (212-922-0123).
> 140 E. 45th Street, 43rd Floor
> New York, NY 10017

◆ **Munder Microcap Equity Fund** (800-239-3334).

◆ **Munder Capital Management**
> 480 Pierce Street
> Birmingham, MI 48009

◆ **Oppenheimer Emerging Technology Fund.** Fund manager, Bruce Bartlett (888-470-0862).
> 2 World Trade Center
> New York, NY 10048-0203

◆ **Renaissance Capital.** Management team, Kathleen Shelton Smith, Linda R. Killian, and William K. Smith (888-IPO-FUND).
> IPO Aftermarket Fund
> 325 Greenwich Avenue
> Greenwich, CT 06830

◆ **Robertson Stephens Microcap Growth.** Fund managers, David J. Evans and Rainerio Reyes (800-766-3863).

> P.O. Box 419717
> Kansas City, MO 64141

GENERAL INVESTMENT RESOURCES WITH IPO COVERAGE

WEB AND PRINT RESOURCES

Barron's. A one-year subscription to the print edition of *Barron's* is $145. It has excellent coverage of the IPO market (800-544-0422; www.barrons.com).

> *Barron's*
> 200 Burnett Road
> Chicopee, MA 01020

Bloomberg Personal Finance. This is a newsstand publication for savvy investors. Published by Bloomberg, the publisher of this book (888-432-5820; www.bloomberg.com).

> *Bloomberg Personal Finance* Magazine, Circulation Dept.
> 100 Business Park Drive, P.O. Box 888
> Princeton, NJ 08542-0888

BusinessWeek. A one-year subscription to the printed and online edition costs $54.95 (888-878-5151; www.business week.com).

> *BusinessWeek*
> P.O. Box 421
> Hightstown, NJ 08520

Forbes. In addition to the magazine, the Forbes.com Web site is one of the most informative and comprehensive resources for investors. Watch for articles by Penelope Patsuris, who often covers IPOs (800-888-9896; www.forbes.com).

> *Forbes* Subscriber Service
> P.O. Box 5471
> Harlan, IA 51593-0971

Fortune. On occasion, you will find a story on IPOs here (800-862-3438; www.fortune.com).

> *Fortune*
> P.O. Box 60001
> Tampa, FL 33660-0001

Internet World. You will see an occasional story on a high-tech IPO in *Internet World*. This publication has many stories on the cutting-edge trends of the high-tech world (www.internetworld.com).

Investor's Business Daily. An annual subscription costs $197 (800-831-2525; www.investors.com).

> Investor's Business Daily
> P.O. Box 661750
> Los Angeles, CA 90066

Motley Fool. Motley Fool is a free Web site. You will see a variety of coverage on companies that are going public (www.fool.com).

News.com. News.com is part of c/net, which is an online content company. This Web site focuses primarily on the high-tech sector. You will see a variety of stories on IPOs (www.news.com).

TheStreet.com. The mastermind of TheStreet.com is the outspoken James J. Cramer. The "Companies" section is where you will find analysis of IPOs—and the analysis is always strong and engaging. A subscription is free (www.thestreet.com).

The Wall Street Journal. The bible of all serious investors. An annual subscription costs $175. Or you can subscribe to the online edition for $59 per year; $29 if you are a subscriber to the printed version (800-JOURNAL; www.wsj.com).

> Dow Jones Publications
> 84 2nd Avenue
> Chicopee, MA 01020

Wired News. This site often contains IPO coverage. The focus, of course, is on high-tech companies (www.wired.com).

OTHER ONLINE RESOURCES FOR INVESTORS

Investor Guide	www.investorguide.com
The New York Times	www.nytimes.com
Upside	www.upside.com

CHAT ROOMS AND DISCUSSION GROUPS

Motley Fool	www.fool.com
Raging Bull	www.ragingbull.com
Stock Chat	www.stockchat.com
Stock Club	www.stockclub.com
Stockmaster	www.stockmaster.com
Stock-Talk	www.stocktalk.com
Yahoo! Finance	www.quote.yahoo.com

INVESTMENT CLUBS

AN INVESTMENT CLUB can be a good resource for information and education. According to the National Association of Investors Corporation (NSIC), investment clubs have consistently outperformed the general market. A club will usually meet, say, once a month and cover a new topic each time. One topic could be IPOs. Sometimes a club will also invite guest speakers (810-583-6242).

To get further information on investment clubs, you can contact the NSIC:

> 711 West Thirteen Mile Road
> Madison Heights, MI 48071

NOTES

CHAPTER 2

1 Larrie A. Weil, telephone conversations with the author, May 1998.

CHAPTER 4

2 Mark Spitzer, e-mail interview by the author, July 1998.

CHAPTER 6

3 Steve Harmon, e-mail interview by the author, May 1998.

CHAPTER 7

4 Harmon.

CHAPTER 8

5 Nadine Wong, e-mail interview by the author, June 1998.

6 Wong.

7 Wong.

8 Wong.

9 Wong.

CHAPTER 12

10 Linda Killian, e-mail interview by the author, May 1998.

11 Killian.

12 Killian.

CHAPTER 13

13 Tom Stewart-Gordon, e-mail interview by the author, July 1998.

14 Drew Field, e-mail interview by the author, July 1998.

15 Stewart-Gordon.

16 Stewart-Gordon.

17 Field.

CHAPTER 14

18 Patrick J. Cusatis, James A. Miles, and J. Randall Woolridge, "Restructuring Through Spinoffs," *Journal of Financial Economics* (Spring 1993): 105-169.

19 Cusatis, Miles, and Woolridge.

GLOSSARY

Absorbed. The condition of an IPO that has been sold out.

Accounts payable. The money a company owes to its creditors, such as for raw materials, inventory, equipment, services, and taxes.

Accounts receivable. Money owed to a company by customers. If accounts receivable are increasing much more than sales, the company may be having problems collecting payments.

Accredited investor. A person who has a net worth of at least $1 million or has an annual income of $200,000 per year. These guidelines are set by federal regulations. It is typically accredited investors who put money into companies that have yet to go public. Because of the high income requirements, many individual investors do not participate in pre-IPO investments.

Agreement among underwriters. A document stating the number of shares to be allocated among the co-managers and syndicate underwriters and enumerating the compensation breakdown.

Allotment. The amount of IPO stock allocated to each underwriter.

American depositary receipt (ADR). A foreign company traded on a U.S. stock exchange. In most cases, ADRs are major companies.

Aftermarket performance. An indication of how well stock has performed after it has gone public. The gain or loss is measured against the offering price.

All or none. A condition providing that if a minimum amount of capital is not raised, an underwriter can cancel the offering. This is usually the case with best-effort offerings, not firm-commitment offerings.

Analyst. A person who researches companies in a certain industry. Analysts work for brokerages, banks, underwrit-

angel

ers, or other financial institutions. Because typical IPOs are small, usually only a few analysts cover an IPO company.

Application service provider (ASP). Technologies are crucial for most companies but also expensive and difficult to maintain. To help companies with these problems, application service providers (ASPs) have been created to outsource technologies. For this service, a client company typically pays a monthly fee, similar to renting software.

Arbitration. A process in which two opposing sides resolve a dispute instead of going to court. Most brokerage accounts require arbitration.

Balance sheet. A list of assets, liabilities, and equity of a company at a certain point in time. The balance sheet is included in a company's prospectus and is a valuable tool for analysis.

Bedbug letter. A notification sent by the SEC to a company to withdraw its IPO offering because the registration statement is not in accordance with the securities laws.

Best-efforts offering. An agreement stating that an underwriter will use its best efforts to sell shares of a company to the public. There is no guarantee of a minimum amount of capital for the issuer. Small companies normally use best-effort underwriters.

Blank-check offering. An IPO that has yet to indicate the type of business it will enter. This kind of IPO is extremely risky.

Block. A large amount of stock—10,000 shares or more. Institutions purchase IPOs in blocks.

Blue-sky laws. State regulations for IPOs.

Book. Information maintained by an underwriter to track all buy and sell orders for a public offering.

Bought deal. *See* Firm-commitment offering.

Break issue. An IPO that falls below the offering price.

Bridge financing. A loan to a company in anticipation of an IPO. Part of the proceeds of the IPO will then be used to pay off the bridge loan. This is a relatively common practice.

Business-to-business (B2B). Two companies conducting

business with each other. Companies are starting to use the Internet to help with this process. For example, an auto manufacturer may use an online exchange to bid for chemical supplies. There are a variety of software companies that provide B2B solutions, such as Ariba and CommerceOne.

Calendar. *See* Pipeline.

Capitalization. The amount of equity and debt a company has.

Cheap stock. Common stock issued to certain people—usually executives and other employees—at prices much lower than what the public will pay.

Classified stock. Types of stock, such as Class A and Class B. The former includes voting rights and is retained by the founders of the company, and the latter is issued to the public.

Clearing price. The price at which the demand for and supply of shares is equalized. A new form of IPO distribution, called OpenIPO, uses an auction system that allows for IPOs to be distributed at the clearing price.

Collar. The lowest price acceptable to an issuer for an IPO.

Commissions. The biggest expense for an IPO. The commissions are what the underwriters and stockbrokers make from the IPO.

Completion. The completion of all IPO trades, which takes about five days from the start of trading. Before completion, an IPO can be canceled and the money returned to investors.

Comfort letter. A letter from an independent auditor stating that the disclosures in the registration statement are correct.

Confirm. Correspondence sent to a client that gives details about a trade, such as the quantity, name of the security, price, and commission.

Cooling-off period. The period of time between the filing of a preliminary prospectus with the Securities and Exchange Commission and the offering of stock to the public.

Current assets. Corporate assets such as cash, government bonds, accounts receivable, and inventory, that can be converted into cash in a year or less. Thus, current assets are an indicator of the liquidity of a company. After an IPO, a company will usually have a high amount of current assets, because of the large infusion of cash from the offering.

Current liabilities. Corporate liabilities that come due within a year or less, such as accounts payable, wages, taxes owed, or interest payments.

Current ratio. A company's current assets divided by its current liabilities. As a general rule, a current ratio of 2:1 shows that a company can meet its debts.

Date of issue. The date upon which an IPO begins trading on the open market.

Deal flow. The frequency at which an underwriter brings companies public.

Dilution. The weaker equity value of the IPO stock compared to that of earlier company shares, due to the increase in both the number of shares and the cost per share.

Direct public offering (DPO). Selling stock directly to the public without using an underwriter, a frequent practice of small companies that have difficulty raising capital. The success rate of DPOs has not been good, although the Internet might change that situation. A major problem with DPOs is lack of liquidity (that is, difficulty selling shares at a good price).

Discount broker. A brokerage firm that charges investors low commission rates. However, a discount broker will typically not provide any investment advice. Recently, discount brokers have been offering their clients the opportunity to invest in IPOs.

Discretionary account. The right of a broker to make transactions in a client account without authorization. This requires a signed power of attorney.

Dividend. A cash payment paid to shareholders, usually on a quarterly basis. However, since IPOs are usually small, dividends may not accrue.

Due diligence. An investigation of an issuer by the underwriter to determine the value of the company.

Eating stock. An underwriter buying IPO stock for its own account because there is not enough demand in the open market. This is a very bad sign for an IPO.

EDGAR. A comprehensive collection of the SEC filings from public companies. There are also prospectuses on EDGAR. You can access the site (www.sec.gov) for free. This is an extremely valuable tool for IPO analysis.

Effective date. The date on which the Securities and Exchange Commission allows a company to issue its shares to the public.

Elephant. A large institutional investor.

E-tailer. An online company that sells products through a Web site, such as Amazon.com.

Financial statements. The balance sheet, income statement, and statement of cash flows for a company, all of which are disclosed in the prospectus.

Firm-commitment offering. An underwriter writes a check to the issuer for a specified number of shares. The underwriter expects to sell these shares to the public at a higher price, thus generating a profit.

Flipping. Investors taking a quick profit when an IPO's value increases at the start of trading. Underwriters do not like flipping, since it places heavy selling pressure on the stock price.

Float. The number of shares the general public owns. Float does not include the stock the insiders own.

Flotation cost. The cost of issuing new stock to the public.

Full-service broker. The traditional stockbroker, who provides financial advice but charges much higher fees than discount brokers. In most cases, it is full-service brokers who sell IPOs, although that situation is changing.

Fully distributed. An IPO that was fully sold to the public.

Going concern. Before a company goes public, an auditor investigates the company's financial data. If the auditor has substantial doubts about a company's ability to continue operating, it will indicate this in the company's prospectus by using the phrase "going concern," which should be a red flag for investors.

Going public. *See* Initial public offering.

Green shoe (also known as an *overallotment option*). An agreement allowing an underwriter to increase the number of shares issued on an IPO. The typical amount is 15 percent of the amount of the issue. A green-shoe option is usually included when an IPO generates high demand.

Group sales. Block sales to institutional investors.

Hot issue. An IPO that trades at a substantial premium on the offering.

House of issue. *See* Lead underwriter.

Income statement. A document showing a company's revenues and expenses. An income statement shows profits or losses and is a required disclosure in a company's prospectus.

Incubator. A holding company that invests in and supports the growth of emerging companies. Examples of such companies include idealab! and CMGI. Incubators generate profits by either selling their portfolio companies or taking them public.

Indication of interest (IOI). A statement from an investor indicating how many shares he or she will buy of an offering. An underwriter collects the IOIs and determines the demand for the offering in order to set an appropriate price and number of shares to be issued.

Initial public offering (IPO). A company selling stock to the public for the first time. Money from the offering can either go into the company or pay off existing shareholders—or a combination of the two.

Insider. A person who is an officer, director, or owner of 10 percent or more of a company. In terms of an IPO, there are a variety of restrictions on how much stock an insider can sell.

Institutional investor. A firm that trades substantial amounts of stock and other investments. Institutions include mutual funds, pensions, banks, and insurance companies.

Investment banker. *See* Underwriter.

Issue. The stock sold by a company in an IPO.

Issuer. The company that is doing an IPO.

Lead underwriter (also known as a *lead manager*). An investment bank, such as Goldman Sachs or CS First Boston, that determines the price of an IPO and how many shares should be allocated to members of the underwriting syndicate.

Liquidity. The ability to turn an asset (such as a stock) into cash quickly without suffering any loss of real value. For small IPOs, there may not be much liquidity.

Lockup period. The 180 days after a company goes public during which officers and insiders are restricted from selling stock.

Managing underwriter. *See* Lead underwriter.

Market makers. Professionals who buy and sell stock for their own accounts and make profits on the difference between their purchase and the selling price (called the *markup*). Strong market makers are crucial for an IPO. After the IPO, the market makers provide liquidity for investors to buy and sell the issue.

Mutual fund. A pool of capital with which money managers invest in stocks and bonds. Investors can purchase shares in the mutual fund. The biggest buyers of IPOs are mutual funds.

NASD (National Association of Securities Dealers). A self-regulatory agency for the securities industry. The NASD tries to ensure fair compensation and trading practices for brokers and underwriters.

Nasdaq (National Association of Securities Dealers Automated Quotation System; also called the *National Market System*). A stock exchange that does not have a physical trading floor. Rather, the Nasdaq trading system is a huge network of phones and computers. Most of the companies that go public will be listed on the Nasdaq exchange.

Net income. The difference between a company's revenues and expenses. If there is a gain, the company has a net profit; if there is a loss, the company has a net loss.

Network effect. A concept that shows the power of certain technologies, such as the telephone. For example, one telephone by itself has zero value, but when a second one is added, there is value. If a third telephone is added, a network is created, and value increases even more. In other words, the more participants in the network, the more valuable the technology. This has happened with a variety of Internet technologies, including free e-mail.

New issue. *See* Initial public offering.

Offering. *See* Initial public offering.

Offering circular. *See* Prospectus.

Offering date. The date of the IPO.

Offering price. The price that the lead underwriter determines for an IPO. This is the price that the original investors get (usually, it is high net worth individuals and institutions who can buy at the offering price).

Opening price (also known as the *first-trade price*). The price at which an IPO starts trading on the open market. In many cases, the price will be at a premium to the offering price.

Oversubscribed. When an IPO has more buyers than there are shares. Most offerings will have a *green-shoe option*, which allows the underwriter to increase the number of shares of the offering if it is oversubscribed. An oversubscribed offering is a good sign and typically means the IPO will trade at a premium on the opening.

Penalty bid. A fee charged by an underwriter if investors flip an issue. That is, a penalty bid is meant to curtail flipping, a practice that can put pressure on the stock price.

Pink Sheets. Companies too small to be listed on Nasdaq. The National Quotation Bureau publishes the stock quotes of Pink Sheets. The Pink Sheets market tends to be very illiquid.

Pipeline. Companies that have filed to do IPOs but have yet to trade.

Preferred stock. Equity in a company whose owners get dividends before common stockholders, as well as preference in the event of liquidation because of bankruptcy. An IPO is usually in the form of common stock, not preferred stock. Rather, preferred stock is normally issued to venture capitalists before a stock is offered to the public.

Preliminary prospectus. *See* Red herring.

Premium (also known as *pop*). The difference between the offering price and opening price of an IPO.

Private placement. The sale of stock or debt to raise money for a company. However, the securities are sold not to the public but instead to high net worth investors and institutions.

Prospectus. A document filed with the Securities and Exchange Commission for companies that want to do an IPO. The prospectus is for investors and discloses all material information, such as risk factors, financial data, management, use of proceeds, and strategies.

Public offering. *See* Initial public offering.

Public offering price. *See* Offering price.

Qualified purchaser. An individual who has a net worth of at least $5 million or who is responsible for net investments of at least $25 million. Qualified-purchaser status is required for certain types of private investments, such as those offered by the online financial firm WR Hambrecht + Co.

Quiet period. The period after a company files its S-1 registration statement during which management is not allowed to make any statements that are not included in the prospectus. The purpose of the quiet period is to prevent the hyping of the IPO. The quiet period lasts until twenty-five days after the stock starts trading.

Real estate investment trust (REIT). A company that invests in real estate properties. If the REIT meets certain federal requirements, it can take advantage of a variety of tax exclusions.

Red herring (also known as the *preliminary prospectus*). A document filed with the Securities and Exchange Commission before the completed prospectus is filed. It's called a red herring because the front page is in red ink and indicates that certain information (such as the number of shares to be issued and the price) is subject to change.

Registration statement. A document consisting of the

prospectus (which is available to the public) and a statement for additional information (which is only for the SEC) that is filed with the SEC. Different types of registration statements include an S-1 and an SB-2.

Regulation A offering. A stock offering for a small company. The maximum amount that can be raised is $5 million. Some companies use the Internet to do Regulation A offerings, but the success rate of these has been low.

Regulation D. A filing that outlines details of a private placement. This is a small offering—usually no more than $5 million—for accredited investors, who have high incomes and net worth. With Regulation D offerings, a company does not have to file disclosures with the Securities and Exchange Commission.

Restricted stock. Stock granted to executives, employees, and private investors of the company before the company goes public. This stock is not registered with the SEC and must comply with a variety of regulations. Typically, this stock cannot be sold until two years after it was granted.

Road show. Visits of senior management to a variety of brokerages to give a presentation to potential investors. Typically, the road shows will be in the major investment centers, such as New York City, San Francisco, and Los Angeles.

SEC. *See* Securities and Exchange Commission.

Securities Act of 1933. The law that covers the regulations for the IPO market.

Secondary offering. A stock issue after a company has already done an IPO.

Securities and Exchange Commission (SEC). The federal agency that regulates securities such as IPOs and insider trading.

Self-underwriting. A company bypassing the use of an underwriter and doing its own offering. Small companies frequently underwrite themselves, with the size of the offering, in most case, below $5 million. However, the success of these types of offerings has been spotty.

Selling stockholders. The officers or founders of an IPO company selling some or all of their positions. Heavy selling may indicate the IPO will not do well.

S-1. A document filed with the Securities and Exchange Commission. The filing includes the prospectus, which is also known as the *registration statement.*

Spinning. A controversial practice in which underwriters give certain high-level officers stock in "hot" IPOs to potentially get future underwriting business.

Spin-off. A subsidiary of a company becoming a separate company via a new stock offering. The stock is usually issued to shareholders of the parent company.

Stabilization. A lead underwriter intervening in the market by buying shares to prevent the stock from falling below its public offering price. This practice protects the stock and is therefore allowed by the SEC.

Sticky deal. An IPO that will be difficult to sell.

Syndicate. A group of underwriters who will sell the offering to investors. IPOs are typically very large, requiring numerous underwriters. The syndicate is headed by the lead manager.

Tombstone. An advertisement for an IPO placed by the lead underwriter.

Tracking stock. A publicly traded security issued by a parent company to track the performance and/or earnings potential of a subsidiary. Or when a major company splits off a division to shareholders, which is what AT&T did when it created a tracking stock for its wireless division. However, a tracking stock is very different from a spin-off; with a tracking stock, the parent company retains much control.

Underwriter. A firm that helps companies do an IPO.

Use of proceeds. A section in a company's prospectus that indicates what it will do with the money from an IPO.

Venture capital (VC). Cash from firms accepted before a company goes public. The venture capital firms usually take a large position in the company.

Waiting period. The period of time between the filing of the registration statement and the time when the shares can be offered to the public.

INDEX

Accounts payable, 81
Accounts receivable, 80, 251
Accumulated deficit, 82
ActivCard SA (ACTI), 4
Activity ratios, 250–252
Aether Systems Inc. (AETH), 128
Affymetrix (AFFX), 139
Agilent Technologies, 217
Agile Software (AGIL), 120
Akamai Technologies Inc., 22, 24,
    28,124
Alert-IPO, 56, 254
Allen, Paul, xvii, 225
Amazon.com Inc. (AMZN), 21, 23,
    118
American Depositary Receipts,
    172–173
America Online (AOL), 93
Ameritrade, 205
Amgen, 136–137, 140
Analysts, 103, 105–106
Apple Computer, 16–17, 89
Application service providers,
    126–127
Ariba (ARBA), 126
Arrowpoint Communications
    (ARPT), 17
Arthur Andersen, 25
ASD Group Inc. (ASDG), 89
Asiacontent.com (IASIA), 172
Assets, current and noncurrent,
    80–81
AT&T, 23, 122, 123, 214, 215
AT&T Wireless (AWE), 216
Attorneys, role of, 25
Auditors, role of, 24–25
Auriana, Lawrence, 188, 189

Bailout, 18, 72
Balance sheet, 79–82
Banking, 147–150
Barron Chase Securities, 96
Barron's, 51, 258
Ben & Jerry's, 206
Benchmark Capital, 21, 205

Berners-Lee, Tim, 22
Biacore International (BCORY),
    140
Biestman, Mark, 104
BioReliance (BREL), 140
Biotechnology IPOs
    analyzing, 136–138
    current and future prospects,
        142–143
    diversity in, 138–140
    factors behind the growth of,
        134
    FDA approval, role of, 135–136
    strategies for investing in,
        140–141
Blockbuster Video, 162
Bloomberg IPO Index, 53
Bloomberg IPO Index Movers, 53
Blue-sky laws, 34
Blumenthal, Robin Goldwyn, 51
Bollenbach, Stephen, 218
Boston Market, 164–165
Brav, Alon, 20–21
Broadcast.com, 106–107
Broadcom, 123
Brokerages, 152–154
    description of online, 195–205
    direct public offerings versus,
        205–209
Brookham Technology (BKHM), 4
B2Bstores.com (BTBC), 92
Buffett, Warren, 7, 100, 154,
    232–233
Bulletin Board, 41
Burger King, 163
Business-to-business (B2B),
    125–126
BusyBox.com (BUSY), 96
Buy.com, 91
Buying IPOs, timing of, 106–107
Buying on margin, 110–111

Calculation of registration fee,
    71–72
California Financial Holding Co.,

209
Caliper Technologies Corp.
    (CALP), 139
Capital resources, 76
Capital stock, 82
Cascade Communications Corp., 2,
    3
CBS Marketwatch-DBCC, 56–57,
    254
Celerity Systems (CLTY), 93–94
Cell Pathways (CLPA), 136
Center Watch, 140
Cerent, 23
Chase Capital Partners, 21
Chat rooms, 63, 260
Chervitz, Darren, 57
chinadotcom corp. (CHINA), 172
Cisco Systems Inc., 17, 21, 23, 41,
    118
CMGI Inc. (CMGI), xvi, 23, 24
CNET, 225
Cold calls, 64
Collateral Therapeutics (CLTX),
    139
Commerce One Inc. (CMRC), 104
Compaq Computer, 88–89
Competition, as a risk factor, 95–96
Coryell, Kirby, 104
Costs of doing IPOs, 18–19
Covad Communications (COVD),
    23
Covering short position, 109
Cramer, James J., 51
CriticalPath (CPTH), 21
CS First Boston, 176
Cyber Force, 207

David's Bridal (DABR), 161–162
Debt ratio, 253
Defaults, 96–97
Dell Computer, 41, 118
Deloitte & Touche, 25
Depreciation, 80
Deshpande, Gururaj, 2–3
Digex Inc. (DIGX), 196
DigitalThink (DTHK), 5, 203–204
Dilution, 76
Direct public offerings (DPOs)
    problems with, 206–209
    versus online, 205–206
Dividend policy, 75
DLJ (Donaldson, Lufkin & Jen-

rette), 195, 196
DLJdirect, 196
Doerr, John, 21
Dollar-cost averaging, 186
Donchess, Charles, 104
DoubleClick, 16
drkoop.com (KOOP), 4, 90, 92
drugstore.com (DSCM), 21
Duane Reade, 162
Due diligence, 34

eBay (EBAY), 90
eChapman.com (ECMN), 243
EDGAR
    Online, 53, 61–62, 256
    resources, 59–62, 256–257
Effective date, 42
Einstein/Noah Bagel Corp.
    (ENBC), 227
Electronic Data Interchange
    (EDI), 125
Ellison, Lawrence, 17
E-Loan Inc. (EELN), 156–157
eMachines (EEEE), 88–89
E*Offering, 200–202
Epicor Software Corp. (EPIC), 21
Epoch, 205
Equity, 82
Ernst & Young, 25
E-tailers, 224–226
eToys, 225–226
E*TRADE, 153, 154, 195, 200
Exchange ratio, 213
Excite, 52
Excite@Home Networks, 21

Fads, 163
    examples of, 224–228
    when to get out, 228
FASTNET Corp. (FSST), 4
FBR.com, 204–205
FDA, role of, 135–136, 140–141
FedEx, 118
Fidelity, 7, 152
Field, Drew, 208, 209
Filo, David, 18
Financial Accounting Standards
    Board, 77
Financial IPOs
    banking, 147–150
    brokerages, 152–154
    insurance, 154–156

mutual funds, 150–152
online services, 156–157
Financial statements, 78–82,
  250–253
Firstworld Communications, Inc.
  (FWIS), 4
Flipping, 5–6, 106
Foreign markets
  how to invest in, 172–173,
    175–177
  popular IPOs, 172
  risk factors, 173–175
  trends in, 169–171
  Web sites for some stock ex-
    changes, 176
Forrester Research, 125, 153
Fosback, Norman, 62
FreeEDGAR, 61, 256–257
Front-running, 177

Gabelli Asset Management (GBL),
  151
Garage.com, xvi
Gartner Group, 127
Gates, Bill, xvii, 120
Gateway Computer, 118
Generally accepted accounting
  principles (GAAP), 77
Genzyme, 140
GoAmerica (GOAM), 128
Going concern, 92
Goldman Sachs, 24, 26, 146, 205
Gompers, Paul, 20–21
Gross margins, negative, 90–91

Hambrecht, William R., xv, 5, 202
Hambrecht & Quist, 24, 202
WR Hambrecht + Co., 202–205
Hampshire Securities, 94
H&Q IPO and Emerging Company
  Fund, 184–185, 189–190
Happiness Express, 227–228
Harmon, Steve, 106, 120
Healtheon Corp. (HLTH), 21
Healthgate Data Corp. (HGAT), 4
Hedging, 174
Hertz, 40
Hewlett-Packard, 217
Hoffman, Mark, 104
Home Depot, 102, 160
Home Shopping Network (HSN),
  223

Homestore.com (HOMS), 21
Hoover, 53, 54
Hot IPO, 106
Human Genome Project, 134, 138

ImproveNet, Inc. (IMPV), 4, 129
Incentive stock options (ISOs),
  235–236
Income statement, 78–79
Incubators, 24
Incyte Genomics, Inc., 138
Insurance IPOs, 154–156
Insweb Corp. (INSW), 157
Intel, 41, 118
Intel Capital, 23
Interactive Products and Services,
  207
International Data Corp., 127–128
International Harvester, 6
Internet Capital Group (ICGE), 5
Internet Scanner, 16
Internet Services Systems (ISS), 16,
  17–18
Internet Stock Report, 51
Intuit Inc. (INTU), 21
Investment Company Institute
  (ICI), 150
Investment strategies
  analysts, listening to, 103,
    105–106
  buying on margin, 110–111
  invest in what you know, 102
  market potential, determining,
    105
  mutual fund holdings, use of,
    103
  neighborhood, 100–102
  researching management, 104
  short selling, 107–110
  venture-backed IPOs, 103–104
Investment Technology Group
  (ITG), 200
Investors, securing, 38–40
IPO Central, 53–54, 255
IPO.com, 58, 254–255
IPO Data Systems, 55–56
IPO Express, 61
IPOfn (financial network), 58–59
IPO Frontline, 58–59
IPO Maven, 57–58, 255
IPO Monitor, 54–55, 255–256
IPO Plus Aftermarket Fund (IPO

Fund), 182–183, 188
IPOs (initial public offerings)
  defined, 14
  reasons for doing, 15–18
  reasons for not doing, 18–20
  the top and the worst, list of, 4
IPO Spotlight, 57

Jenna Lane (JLNY), 88
John Hancock Financial Services,
  Inc.,155
Johnson, Walter E., 149
Journal of Finance, 20
Juniper Networks Inc. (JNPR), 21,
  27, 104
Jupiter Communications, 128

Kaplan, Stanley, 88
Karger, David, 22
Kaufman Fund, 188–189, 257
Killian, Linda R., 183, 184, 188
Klaus, Christopher, 16, 17
Klein, Andrew, 197–198
Kleiner Perkins Caufield & Byers,
  21, 205
KPMG, 25
Krispy Kreme Doughnuts Inc., 164
Krizelman, Todd, 88

Lauer, John, 233
Lawsuits, 88–89
Legato (LGTO), 97
Leighton, Tom, 22
Letter of intent, 34–36
Lewin, Danny, 22
Liabilities, current and noncur-
  rent, 81
Limit order, 199
Liquidity, 17–18, 76, 250
Livermore, Jesse, 107
Lockup provision, 78, 107, 185
Lucent, 214, 215
Lycos (LCOS), 21
Lynch, Peter, 7, 100, 152

MacKay, Charles, 222
Maggs, Bruce, 22
Manhattan Bagel, 227
Managers/management teams
  importance of, 120
  of mutual funds, 185–186, 187
  researching, 104

as a risk factor, 86–88
Margin, buying on, 110–111
Marine Management Systems,
  96–97
Marriott, 214
Marsico, Tom, 151
Martha Stewart Living Omnimedia,
  21, 164
Marvell Technology Group Ltd., 4
Maxygen (MAXY), 142
May Department Stores, 162
McDonald's, 163, 165, 224
Menlow, David, 57
Merrill Lynch, 227
Metropolitan Life Limited (MET),
  155
Microsoft Corp., 16, 17, 41, 118,
  120
Minkow, Barry, 108
Molecular Dynamics (MDYN), 140
Moore, Gordon, 116
Moore's Law, 116–117
Morgan Stanley, 24, 35, 176, 205
Mortgage.com Inc. (MDCM), 156
Motley Fool, 52, 259
Munder Microcap Equity Fund,
  189, 257
Mutual funds, IPO, 103, 150–152,
  257–258
  advantages of, 184–186
  description of specific, 188–190
  fees, types of, 185
  strategies of, 196–187
MySimon.com, 225

Nacchio, Joseph, 123
Nasgovitz, William, 100
National Association of Securities
  Dealers (NASD), 37, 40–41
NationsBanc Montgomery Securi-
  ties, 87
NaviSite (NAVI), 127
Net income, 79
Netscape, 119, 232
Network Solutions Inc. (NSOL),
  18
Neuberger Berman Inc. (NEU),
  151
New Focus Inc. (NUFO), 4
Newsletters, 62, 257
New World Coffee-Manhattan
  Bagels Inc. (NWCI), 227

New York Stock Exchange (NYSE), 40, 41
NextCard Inc. (NXCD), 157
Nokia, 23
Nuance Communications Inc., 4, 5, 199

Oakley IPO, 5
O'Connor, Kevin, 16, 17–18
Offering price, 42
    initial public, 71–72
OpenIPO, xv, 202–203
Oppenheimer Enterprise, 190
Oracle (ORCL), 7, 17, 21, 23, 41
Oracle Ventures, 23–24
Orchid Biosciences, Inc. (ORCH), 4
Over-allotment option, 72
Over-the-counter (OTC) market, 40

Palm Inc., 217, 243
Parexel (PRXL), 140
Paternot, Stephen, 88
Paxson, Lowell, 223
Pennsylvania Railroad, 7
Penny stock, 96
Peritus Software Services (PTUS), 86–87
PerSeptive Biosystems (PBIO), 140
Peterson, Brad, 205
Pets.com, Inc. (IPET), 4, 129
P.F. Chang's China Bistro Inc. (PFCB), 164
Phone.com, 128
Pink Sheets, 41
Planet Hollywood IPO, 5, 226
Price, Michael, 7, 150
Price-earnings ratio, 252–253
Price of issue, 35
Pricewaterhouse Coopers, 25
Printers, financial, 26
Privacy, loss of, 20
Prospectuses, 36
    obtaining, 68
Prospectuses, parts of
    business, 76–77
    certain transactions, 77–78
    company section, 73–74
    dilution, 76
    dividend policy, 75
    financial statements, 78–82

front page, 71–73
liquidity and capital resources, 76
management, 77
plain-English rules for drafting, 70
qualification requirements, 73
quarterly financial results, 76
risk factors, 74–75
sections of, 70–71
shares eligible for future sale, 78
use of proceeds, 75
Proxy statements, 187
Public relations firms, 26–27
Puma Technology (PUMA), 21

Qualcomm, 119
Qualix Group, 97
Quantum Effect Devices, Inc. (QEDI), 4
Quest Software (QSFT), 120
Quick & Reilly, 152, 194
Quiet period, 40
Qwest Communications (Q), 123

Real estate investment trusts (REITs), 75
Real Goods Trading, 207
RealNetworks Inc. (RNWK), 119–120
Red Hat (RHAT), 21, 205
Red herring, 38–39
Red Herring, 52, 256
Reebok, 224
Registrar, 27–28
Registration statement, 36–38
Regulation A, 208
Regulation D, 201
Renaissance Capital, 182–184, 257
Retail IPOs, 160–165
Retained earnings, 82
Risk factors, 74–75
    business model, 90
    competition, 95–96
    default on indebtedness, 96–97
    in foreign markets, 173–175
    going concern, 92
    inexperienced management, 86–88
    limited history of profitability, 92–94

litigation pending, 88–89
low-priced stock, 96
market and customer base, 89
negative gross margins, 90–91
operational systems, 91–92
transition to a new business
    model, 97
Road show, 38
Rockwell Medical Technologies,
    90–91
Rule 504, 208
Ryles, Scott, 205

Sakamoto, Ross, 189
Satyam Infoway (SIFY), 172
SB-1 and SB-2, 37, 71
Charles Schwab, xvii, 152, 152–153,
    176, 194, 195, 205
Scoop, 129
Securities Act (1933), 33
Securities and Exchange Commis-
    sion (SEC), 33, 59, 70. See
    also EDGAR
    commons disclaimer, 72, 73
    Cyber Force, 207
Securities Exchange Act (1934), 33
Seelig, Jonathan, 22
Sequoia Capital, 21
Shah, Manish, 57
Shochet Holding Corp. (SHOC), 4
Short selling, 107–110
Silicon Investor, 52
SkyMall (SKYM), 93
SmartMoney, 51
Smith, Dan, 3
Smith, Fredrick, 225
Smith, Kathleen, 184
Smith, Randall, 50
Smith, Vince, 120
Smith, William, 184
Snapple, 228
Software, 121–122
S-1, 37, 71
Sonus Networks Inc. (SONS), 4, 5,
    105
Soros, George, 108
Soundview Technology Group, Inc.,
    199
Southwest Bancorporation of Tex-
    as, 149
Spam, 63–64
Spinning, 36

Spin-offs
    defined, 212
    equity carve-out, 214
    finding good, 217–218
    reasons for, 215
    recent, 217
    split-off, 214–216
    tracking stock, 216
    traditional, 213–214
Spitzer, Mark, 76
Split-offs, 214–216
Spring Street Brewery, 197–198
Sprint, 216
Stamps.com (STMP), 23
Starbucks, 160, 163
StarMedia (STRM), 21
Steinhardt, Michael, 108
Stewart-Gordon, Tom, 206, 208
Stock appreciation rights (SARs),
    237
Stockbrokers, 63
Stock options
    basics of, 234–235
    guidelines, 237–239
    pros and cons of, 232–233
    types of, 235–237
Stocks, as currency, 18
StorageNetworks, Inc. (STOR), 4
Strategic investors, 23–24
Sun Life Financial Services (SLC),
    155
Sun Microsystems Inc. (SUNW), 21
Sycamore Networks Inc. (SCMR),
    2–4

TD Waterhouse, 205
Technology IPOs
    application service providers,
        126–127
    business-to-business, 125–126
    factors to look for in, 118–120
    infrastructure, 123–125
    software, 121–122
    telecommunications, 122–123
    wireless, 127–129
Telebras, 169–170
Telecommunications, 122–123
Tenenbaum, Jay, 104
theglobe.com (TGLO), 87–88
ThermaCell Technologies (VCLL),
    94–95
TheStreet.com (TSCM), 51–52,

95–96, 259
3Com, 217
Tombstone ad, 39–40
Topps baseball cards, 228
Toys, as fads, 227–228
Tracey, Jay, 190
Transfer agent, 27–28
Treasury stock, 82
Tribune Co., 23
Trident Capital, 205
Turnstone Systems, Inc. (TSTN), 4

Underwriters, 24, 28–29
    discount, 19
    process, 248–249
United Fruit, 6
United Parcel Service (UPS), 17
U.S. Steel, 7
Uproar Inc. (UPRO), 4
Utsch, Hans, 188, 189

Valentine, Don, 21
Value America (VUSA), 91–92, 225
VarsityBooks.com Inc. (VSTY), 4,
    129
Venture-backed IPOs, 103–104
Venture capitalists, 20–21, 77–78
Venture Law, 234
VeriSign Inc. (VRSN), 18, 35, 125
Vickrey, William, 202
Vostock.com, 200

Wall Street Journal, The, 50–51, 259
Wal-Mart, 102, 160, 161
Walton, Sam, 161
webMethods, Inc. (WEBM), 4,
    71–72, 73
Weil, Larrie, 42
Western Union, 7
Wiggan, Albert, 107
Wired, 26
Wireless, 127–129
Wit Capital, 5, 38, 197–202
Wit SoundView Group, Inc.,
    199–202
Wong, Nadine, 133, 134, 140, 141,
    142
Woolworth's, 7
WorldCom, 170
WR Hambrecht + Co., 202–205
Wynd Communications Corp., 128

Yahoo! (YHOO), 18, 21, 52
Yang, Jerry, 18

ZZZZ Best, 108

ABOUT BLOOMBERG

Bloomberg L.P., founded in 1981, is a global information services, news, and media company. Headquartered in New York, the company has nine sales offices, two data centers, and 80 news bureaus worldwide.

Bloomberg, serving customers in 100 countries around the world, holds a unique position within the financial services industry by providing an unparalleled combination of news, information, and analytic tools in a single package, known as the BLOOMBERG PROFESSIONAL™ service. Corporations, banks, money management firms, financial exchanges, insurance companies, and many other entities and organizations rely on Bloomberg as their primary source of information.

BLOOMBERG NEWSᔆᴹ, founded in 1990, offers worldwide coverage of economies, companies, industries, governments, financial markets, politics, and sports. The news service is the main content provider for Bloomberg's broadcast media, which include BLOOMBERG TELEVISION®—the 24-hour cable and satellite television network available in ten languages worldwide—and BLOOMBERG RADIO™—an international radio network anchored by flagship station BLOOMBERG® WBBR AM1130 in New York.

In addition to the BLOOMBERG PRESS® line of books, Bloomberg publishes *BLOOMBERG® MARKETS, BLOOMBERG PERSONAL FINANCE*™, and *BLOOMBERG® WEALTH MANAGER*. To learn more about Bloomberg, call a sales representative in one of the following cities:

Frankfurt: 49-69-920-410	San Francisco: 1-415-912-2960
Hong Kong: 852-977-6000	São Paulo: 5511-3048-4500
London: 44-171-330-7500	Singapore: 65-438-8585
New York: 1-212-318-2000	Sydney: 61-29-777-8686
Princeton: 1-609-279-3000	Tokyo: 81-3-3201-8900

ABOUT THE AUTHOR

Tom Taulli is a specialist in the initial public offering field and has written about the stock market for a variety of publications, including *Barron's, eCompany Now, Research* magazine, *Individual Investor,* and *Registered Representative.* He also writes columns on IPOs for such online publications as CBS MarketWatch, internet.com, Forbes.com, and Gomez.com. Currently the Internet stock analyst for internet.com, he is a regular on CNBC and CNN and is the author of *Stock Options—Getting Your Share of the Action.*

Venture Capital p/04
Kleiner Perkins
Sequoia
Benchmark Capital

50
98
105

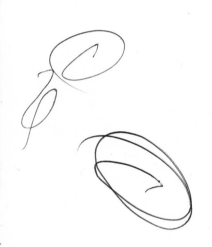

O'Neill
Venture capital 104
p51 - Authors address
135 - FDA - 3

Seq Cap comp p21

Q - Lead Broker - Sponsorship
Venture capital p21
NC Law Firms p25